About the author:

Diane Cordaire had a career as an acting agent in Sydney, Australia. She was also a photographer for 23years. The Lord spoke to her, asking her to give up all to follow Him. She thought she was following Him as she had become a Deacon within the church and had ministries in homelessness and Christian media.

She heard His voice speak again, "Buy a tent." After hearing this voice, she gave away her possessions, career, income and bought a tent. She lived near the rivers of Australia for seven years by herself while writing her first book 'How I Overcame My Own Life.' This time now equates to 12 years of not having an outward place to call home. She still doesn't own any possessions and all that she owns fits into a sports car. Nowadays she's given comfort to write this book in house-sitting accommodations. Her daughters keep a beautiful space available for her when she is back within their reach. But she still carries a tent just in case the Lord takes her beyond the comforts. She found that staying in the rest and trusting God was all she needed, and home was within. His Grace is sufficient!

The journey caused her to reflect on the flaws in her life. To overcome her hereditary hand-me-downs, thoughts, and any hurts collected along the way was the task at hand. This process brought her peace of mind and hope for her future. Her principal goal was to be Holy, just as He is Holy. This book is the path to Holiness that she took.

I hope you enjoy reading!

BORN TO BE HOLY

Diane Cordaire

Born to be Holy

Copyright © 2021 by Diane Cordaire

ISBN XXX X XXXXXXX X X

Book orders or enquiries:

Email: dianecordaire@gmail.com or phone: 0425 258 263

Introduction

To experience life to the fullest takes a lifetime! Endurance, persistence, and long-suffering are the ingredients to understand the instructions or messages brought to us daily as a gift of His Grace and Mercy. To become Holy, we'll incur the pain of His suffering. All of us fall short of His Glory until we become the Glory. That is the task at hand! Most people are born into fundamental thinking, which keeps us on shallow ground or in routine living. Becoming free from the cords of wickedness surrounding our mind is called "overcoming". Once achieved, Holy ground is where we will stand. Holiness is in all who are born upon the earth. That is what He/God-The Creator of the Universe, has called us to become.

Be Holy just as I am Holy - 1 Peter 1:16

Take a walk with me beyond the soul tie of the lie and back into His glorious realm of blessings and promises to reveal the true image of God upon humanity.

Open my eyes to my understanding and awaken the wonder of my imagination beyond what I could hope or think. Let me see the beauty in all that you have created and reflect that beauty into me, so that I can see you in me and me in you.

The first three chapters of this book cover the overcoming process. A stage that life coming out of sin needs to take. The second part of the book is life projected forward as God writes it in His Bible, Revelation. The Bible is inspired by the Holy Spirit in and through people. This book is His projection through me. I pray I saw it correctly.

Chapter 1

Overcoming

Individuals suggested back at the birth of humanity that 'living was a walk in the garden', which it was. Getting back to that place of blessing and perfection is the art of life. To overcome the generational calamities of sins is the beginning of what we can forecast for our walk upon the earth. Unfortunately, our logic becomes polluted and compromised by human thinking over many generations. What we call 'free will' is not free at all.

Adam and Eve lost the original portion of real estate. However, that real estate still lives within all who are born upon the earth. Since that time, we have strayed far into darkness, with only a few making their way back home into the Holy perfection of love.

Returning to the centre of our being is the pearl of great price. We must face our own darkness to allow the light to shine forth. The path of nobility and royalty that only a few will follow is the way forward. The centre of our being is where we will find the image of Christ - becoming unified with Holiness. Emptying our lives of all that once was relevant, such as careers, possessions, image, titles, self-desires, ambitions, comforts, security, and safety will reveal an existence with nothingness. That's where God is to be found!

When Paul was blinded on the road to Damascus, he saw Christ in his nothingness. He became blind so he could see. He saw Christ with his inner eye, not his outer eye. *There is no separation in the Love of God* - Romans 8:31. Humans have separated God from society and out of their bodies and minds. But what people cannot do is divide God from our spirit. God is spirit, and your spirit is the same.

Let them be one just as I am one with the father - 1 John 17:21.

Beyond the darkness is the resurrection and recovery of all things that seem lost. *We need to lose our life to find our life* Matthew - 10:39.

Imagine not judging good or evil but living a life full of all possibilities and potential. To seek beyond individuals and communities' best attainments into the eyes of the Father of heaven and earth would give a different result. This would take a fresh thinking as our mind has undertaken life in a certain way. The new intention becomes the pursuit of perfect love. That original plan for the people on the earth was given by God. In my conclusion, that superb place still lives in us all - we lose nothing until we remember it again. If we are not thinking of that place, we are not pursuing the fullness of love.

The Lord knew us before we were in our mother's womb - Isaiah 44:24.

Recognising that we attached our consciences to darkness back when humans took a bite of the forbidden fruit in the garden of God is such a heavy discovery. Few people will take back what was stolen with the fall of mankind and pursue the highest goal of human endeavour. Holiness!

How do you continue in the light beyond darkness?

Prayer: *"Open my eyes Lord, to the complete works of God for mankind on earth in this lifetime! Let me see beyond my own understanding. Release us from captivity and bring us out of the nations where you sent us. Restore our fortunes to us and bring us home to our own land.*

Let us see what no eye has seen, and no ear has heard."

Most people nowadays have only their own lives in their eyes - they cannot see beyond themselves. Of course, beyond self, we will produce a different result. But we must get to the end of selfishness or ego. Self-expression of talents and ambitions was never ample to finish the task we were called for on this earth.

Many are called few are chosen - Matthew 22:14.

We have two lives functioning at the exact moment within our bodies. Our external world and our inner realm! These two dimensions are grating on each other until one dimension becomes a reality. If good does not triumph, you will live in a world that does not provide happiness. Faith to accept our inner life can process into the exterior world is what brought us to earth to fulfil. *The Kingdom of Heaven is within and the violent take it by* force - Matthew 11:12. This verse claims there is plucking out of heaven into the external creation. Heaven I consider is *'The Kingdom of God',* or our inside realm.

The effective fervent prayers of a righteous man avail much - John 5:16. Fervent means to keep asking until it forms into existence. Violence is fervent! Press through and take back 'The Kingdom of God' and announce it into reality. If you listen to the traitor of your mind, it lies, instructs, controls, and limits your life. Listening to the narrative of the world, you would run short of the glory of God. It is up to us to *"fight the good fight"* and overcome our fallen nature. I've prayed prayers that do not develop into existence. Analysing why they're not answered, I admit I prayed from my selfish ambitions instead of God's hope within.

Your eyes saw my substance, being yet unformed. And in Your book, they all were written, the days fashioned for me, when yet there were none of them - Psalm 139:16.

People in their own eyes think they are doing good. *For now, we see through a glass, darkly; but then face to face; now I know in part: but then shall I know even as also I am known* - 1 Corinthians 13:12.

I observe so many people who are what I would call evil getting blessings - and people who I would claim good not receiving blessings. I have seen God using good to alter evil and evil to repair good. Remembering God owns the keys to heaven and hell so He can apply all elements to ensure not one human should perish.

The Lord is not slack concerning His promise, as some count slackness, but is long suffering toward us, not willing that any should perish but that all should come to repentance - 2 Peter 3:9. It is up to us to pray the prayer of a righteous person. God will overturn the curse within our own bodies.

What is Blessed can't be cursed - Numbers 23:20. It's then up to us to recognise where the devil may plunder us and pray for the curse to be overturned. Going further, *asking for seven times what has been stolen to be returned* - Proverbs 6:21. All was written that He will return what is ours. *A good man leaves an inheritance to his children's children, and the wealth of the sinner is laid up for the just* - Proverbs 13:22. An inheritance can be the spiritual ground you have restored in your family's bloodline. Money and property are not always what an inheritance means.

Concentrating on our bank accounts or economy, we will run short of the completeness of His love and majesty. *The devil roams around looking for who he can devour* - 1 Peter 5:8. Turning your eyes upon the agreement of God will cause the darkness to release what was held up in your life. God says, *No one can serve two masters. Either you will hate the one and love the other, or you will be devoted to the one and despise the other* - Matthew 6:24. I had a dream that I had to withdraw my economy from the world and put my focus into heaven. This alteration caused my concentration to be on Him, not the world.

For where your treasure is, there your heart will be also - Matthew 6:21. It was like taking a needle out of the worldly vein of economy and installing the needle into God's trust. What I encountered when I did this was a heaviness came upon my shoulders. It characterized the world's economy, how it has neglected many of us and it rests upon our shoulders in heaviness.

Come to Me, all you who labour and are heavy laden, and I will give you rest. Take My yoke upon you and learn from Me, for I am gentle and lowly in heart, and you will find rest for your souls. For My yoke is easy and My burden is light - Matthew 11:28-30.

Humanity has been running short for many years. We need help with our understanding to turn it from enough to more than enough. Some individuals have been raised in a privileged lifestyle and handed hope to work with fulfilling their potential. Others battle just to become free of the circumstances they were born into upon the earth. Our forefathers offered us chains and desolation instead of entitlement and inheritance. Beyond our earthly heritage is our heavenly inheritance. *He shall choose our inheritance for us, the excellency of Jacob whom he loved* - Psalm 47:4. Humans who were not born into opportunities find it simpler to relate with our Heavenly Father and draw upon His blessings. And those who were born with privilege find it harder to connect to God's presence.

It is easier for a camel to go through the eye of a needle than for someone who is rich to enter the kingdom of God - Matthew 19:24. Often, we rely on our income or whatever wealth that is handed to us. But there is more: if we rely on our Heavenly Father and His resources from His treasury, *all things are possible for those who believe* - Mark 9:23.

The LORD will send rain at the proper time from his rich treasury in the heavens and will bless all the work you do. You will lend to many nations, but you will never need to borrow from them - Deuteronomy 28:12.

To fulfil scripture, we need to be in the right place within ourselves to receive. Our focus needs to be on Him, not our mission or our future. Then, God's resources will transfer into the potential we carry within our life. Once we have been through the overcoming process, life becomes a shared life here on earth. *And they two shall be one flesh: so, then they are no more two, but one flesh* - Mark 10:8. *But seek the Kingdom of God, and all these things shall be added to you* - Matthew 6:33.

This scripture is saying to put His purpose first. If we think of Him first He will then add the desires of our heart.

Deferred Hope makes the heart sick - Proverbs 13:12. This darkness envelops us, blocking the floodgates of the open heaven. Remember, the kingdom of God is within. How many places in your life have you seen suspended hope? Love, finances, homes, land, opportunities, purpose. The devil has besieged and detained us by delaying hope, and our heart grows sick of waiting. Once recognised that 'deferred hope' has entangled us, we can pray to expect promises fulfilled.

Drop down, ye heavens, from above, and let the skies pour down righteousness: let the earth open, and let them bring forth salvation, and let righteousness spring up together; I the LORD have created it - Isaiah 45:8.

People grow old because of lack of inspiration, and their hope is deferred. This causes them to be tired of living. Staring into a baby's face, they twinkle with excitement, as each moment is inspiring. We forget that wonder and become old in our fundamental routines. This feature of curiosity needs to be renewed in our lives.

Falling in love with life without the encumbrances that have entrapped us, would enable us to become free, and heaven will find us there. In the conclusion, it is not what we possess or give, it's who we grow into that counts. Taking the path of overcoming and loving will produce the greatest rewards.

Do you not know that in a race all the runners run, but only one gets the prize? Run in such a way as to get the prize - 1 Corinthians 9:24.

The aim is love, and love is Christ walking alive on the earth in those who have allowed the overcoming process to transform their understanding and behaviours. Imagine many individuals who have overcome walking with Christ's likeness and virtue upon the earth. That is what many of His people are pursuing to grow into, 'His Bride'. These people appreciate they are bearing Christ's image and Glory, and when the season is perfect, we will see the Glory and righteousness upon them on the earth. They are eager to witness God the Father's plan come about to fulfil their call. It was never about them or their plans. It has always been about God and His plan.

Arise, shine, for your light has come, and the glory of the LORD rises upon you - Isaiah 60:1

Life reaches us on three fronts: the spiritual, physical, and soul realm. The natural physical is to be praised, *for we are fearfully and wonderfully made* - Psalm 139:14. Our divine spirit wants to move and live on the surface physical realm. Our soul or our mind possesses two battles. One requires your spirit's desires - the other wants to interrupt you from growing into all that you were called to be. It's up to us to lean towards the heart of divine *for He knows the plans He has for you, plans to prosper not to harm you* - Jeremiah 29:11. An inward search will reveal what blockages are delaying us from our heart's desire.

If sickness plagues your body, you must learn how to be well by pressing into His promises through faith. Overcoming your mind is like a battlefield. Learn how to bring every thought captive into the will of God. *Casting down imaginations, and every high thing that exalts itself against the knowledge of God and bringing into captivity every thought to the obedience of Christ* - 2 Corinthians 10:15. If you have unbelief, ask Him to help you with your unbelief. *If you can believe, all things are possible to him who believes* - Mark 9:23. Belief and faith propel us to stand adorned in perfect love.

I will come for my bride, that He might present her to Himself a glorious church, not having spot or wrinkle or any such thing, but that she should be holy and without blemish - Ephesians 5:27.

Work out your salvation with fear and trembling - Philippians 2:12.

After years of coming out of the world, I found the 'self' door within myself. The first door that Adam and Eve opened in the soul realm. It's like 'Winey the Poo'. We need to go through the porthole that took us away from that perfect place and took us into the darkness, wilderness, and deserts. All the time wandering, wanting to come back home but not knowing where it is.

Dreams and desires will appear once we have entered through this porthole within our soul. God was always on the other side and could not pour all our dreams and promises into 'self'. If He had poured out his blessings, it would have finished up the same as what we've previously experienced. Abuse!

I grew up in a regular household, Mum and Dad, two children. Dad was a police officer and Mum a security officer. At age thirteen, my Dad left, and my Mum went searching for a new companion. That left me unprotected. I recall wandering into a housing commission avenue with low-income families, to a friend's house. This is where it went wrong for me. I have wandered for fifty years and been abused by the best abusers in the land.

Even though I discovered God at age thirty-six, I was still on the path of the bad economy, and most things ended with a sense of abuse. *God says, and we know all things work together for good to those who love God, to those who are the called according to His purpose* - Romans 8:28. All that we have experienced can work for the Glory of God. We have to find the innocence left behind with the potential that still lives within, and emerge them into God's economy.

As we continue with no other idols before our Lord it gives the results we have desired. God declares, *But seek first his kingdom and his righteousness, and all these things will be added to you* - Matthew 6:33.

Have no other idols before Him - Exodus 20:3. A dream, desire, projects, body, life or promises cannot remain before the King of King and the Lord of Lords. The Israelites wandered in the desert for forty years and the earth opened up and they died. They had idols and refused to give them up, plus they were complainers. Only three people were brought into the Promise Land. This represents promises given by our Lord. We haven't received because we haven't had the Lord first in our eyes.

We are the apple of His eye - Psalm 17:8. Is He the apple of your eyes?

Seek His face - Psalm 27:8. To meet someone face to face, we need to come out of the distractions of the world, society, projects, or whatever is calling our attention. Standing face to face with someone is giving them the time with your presence. Following Jesus Christ is to love His ways. But to see Him face to face is another thing altogether. Wanting to enter His essence and presence takes commitment and determination of choice by faith to manifest what you love.

Prayer: "Open our eyes, Lord, so we can see your face."

Throughout life, we get shut down, put off, and others dictate the standard at which we live. This is not manifesting Christ in the natural. He said, *His righteousness will go before us and His glory will be our rear-guard* - Isaiah 58:8. If we are not expecting His return, we are not in the right place to receive Him. Every generation since Christ's resurrection, a selection of people stood expecting His return. His disciples had their faces like flint towards Him, and they said, *Come Lord Jesus come* - Revelation 22:20. Their only desire was His return.

He decrees, *Then we who are alive, who are left, will be caught up together with them in the clouds to meet the Lord in the air, and so we will always be with the Lord* - 1 Thessalonians 4:17. This gathering is after the tribulation that must take place upon the earth. (I will speak about this in further detail later in this book). *Then the kingdom of heaven will be like ten virgins who took their lamps and went to meet the bridegroom. Five of them were foolish, and five were wise.* Many will miss this wonderful gathering in the air because they won't repent and turn from their sinful ways. Nor did they have the Lord as their focus. The foolish will miss the opportunity! *Look, He is coming in the clouds, and every eye will see Him, even those who pierced Him;*

and all peoples on earth "will mourn because of Him. So, shall it be! Amen - Revelation 1:7.

This great coming is after the bride of Christ has been gathered in the air. Because this bride comes back to reign and rule with Him upon the earth. The virgins with oil in their lamps are the Bride of Christ. They who have made themselves ready to *present to himself as a radiant church, without stain or wrinkle or any other blemish, but holy and blameless* - Ephesians 5:27.

Born To Be Holy

Chapter 2

Looking into Him

Many years of overcoming have brought me into the bridal chamber of my own soul, anticipating the bridegroom's return. When nothing remains before the Lord, and all else has fallen away, that's when you have oil in your lamp. He desires to see us face to face; otherwise He would not have told us to come.

The soul has an upper room and a lower room. The upper room is where the garden of God is, and the lower room is where the distractions of the world live. There is a doorway between the upper and lower. This doorway we opened within the soul when man disobeyed God back at the beginning of time. The idea is to recognise what comes into your day that would take you away from the upper room of your soul. The mind or soul is to be in peace all the time. If you have a war in your mind, you need to deal with that first.

You realise when you have arrived at the upper chamber because you recognise that the expression of who you were, is changing. The delight you felt was shallow, contrasted to the joy you feel when the Lord takes complete custody of the life you have called your own. When we come to the edge of ourselves, that's when we see into the eyes of the one who calls himself the bridegroom.

He is beyond creation and the creatures of the earth. Beyond our understanding and imagination. Beyond our subconscious mind and memory. We then look beyond our eyes into His eyes, and into His existence. Seeing with the eyes of His understanding, new visions of Him and His reality emerge.

Entering His dwelling place is a faith step beyond our anxieties, beyond our living patterns. His dwelling place is the place of rest. All of us have a book we have lived. Some a sad tale, others a rich man's story. Wealthy people rarely think they need God, nor do comfortable people; they are in danger of missing the mark. Whereas individuals who have little or nothing seem to know God! They have come to the place in their story to reach beyond themselves to see God. It is vital in our journey for Holiness to relinquish our story so God can present us with His restored version.

The life in His overcoming bride who has made herself ready, that's His story for you. Individuals can project this miserable story over your life. It's essential to lift the words of condemnation and judgement from yourself. *Therefore, let us stop passing judgment on one another. Instead, make up your mind not to put any stumbling block or obstacle in the way of a brother or sister* - Romans 14:13. It is a simple prayer of faith! You likewise can project this sad story over your life because you get used to living life that way.

There are three stages that the soul needs to pass through before oneness with God becomes a reality. Past times our forefathers have called these stages the dark night of the soul. I call it into the grave to resurrect. Something always has to die before you can get the resurrected version to come to light. Jesus died and we saw His resurrected Glorified body appear before hundreds.

The first stage is the sensual lusts of the world. These senses can develop into passions that lead us away from the focus of God. Examples include: food, carnal passions, people, possessions, careers, comforts, business, entertainment, dreams, money, and technology. I understood desires come from God, but glancing back over my course, I realise they developed from my selfish requests. God told Eve when she accepted the forbidden fruit that she would desire a husband. *Your desire will be for your husband, and he will rule over you"* - Genesis 3:16. This desire is a curse! God granted Adam a wife, she was a gift, not a desire from Adam. I believe desires become pure once we restore our nature back from selfish goals. God says, *Have no other Gods before me* - Exodus 20:3.

Often, we make idols here on earth. *But you shall not make for yourself an idol in the form of anything in the heavens above, on the earth below, or in the waters beneath* - Exodus 20:4. Idols appear in many forms, such as movie stars, sporting events, entertainment personalities, and even preachers can become rock stars in their congregations. These are all idols before God! Idols are pride in the fallen nature. The Israelites had a golden calf image - this was the straw that broke Moses. Moses had been on Mt Sinai receiving the Ten Commandments and when he came down, they confronted him with a golden calf image and were worshipping the image. How many of us calculate our money daily or have a ten-year plan on how to accumulate more possessions? All of this is sensual worldly desires or idols.

The second dark night the soul must pass through - our eyes will be transformed from fallen eyes to renewed vision. This process will welcome us into union with God. Peering through our fallen eyes into the world, we see adversity and sorrow. If you gaze through the eyes of the resurrected Christ, you will see 'Thy Kingdom Come'. Perspective casts vision, and visions are established through our confession.

Declaring the downfall of civilisation, we will see the crashing of the world. But declaring the rebirth of the world, we will see the shift of society as it was written. We can denounce with our comments or we can energise fresh life with faith. This process draws us through to partnership with God. The results will be *Thy kingdom come, thy will be done on earth as it is in heaven* - Matthew 6:10.

God has written that a new Jerusalem will come out of paradise to the earth, adorned as a bride for her husband. Her husband is The Lord Jesus Christ and the bride is the transformed church that has overcome.

Not all who live upon the earth will enjoy this new life that will take place after the tribulation. The tribulation is the calamity of the world and the calling for repentance from the Lord. This period of time lasts seven years and those seven years are divided into two sections. The first section being the time of sorrow, and the second part is the tribulation. Beyond that comes God's wrath poured out upon the remaining people who did not turn from their wicked ways. Once the Lord has cleansed the earth from wickedness, we will reign upon the earth for a thousand years with the Lord. What a time to be born! Very exciting! *If My people who are called by My name will humble themselves, and pray and seek My face, and turn from their wicked ways, then I will hear from heaven, and will forgive their sin and heal their land* - 2 Chronicles 7:14.

The mortal soul has collected many imperfections throughout its lifetime through thoughts and senses. Our bodies carry our soul while on the earth. It takes a mighty effort to lose every string of desire and cast off every yoke within our weakened character. Having one string left behind in your soul connected to a fallen nature will prevent us from piercing the changeover - your will into his will and your mortal body into His resurrected body. A finished work demands to be within our soul; we were produced for His will, not of our own. *Being confident of this, that he who began a good work in you will carry it on to completion until the day of Christ Jesus* - Philippians 1:6.

God dwells within what He calls the tabernacle, and we have called this our body. When we fulfil the complete works of overcoming the deep, powerful presence of Christ's life will stand where we once stood.

There is no victory without loss!

Setting my eyes upon Our Lord Jesus Christ has produced a new day for me. Finally, I can understand the conversion of years of devotion and sacrifice. Staring at Jesus Christ hanging on the cross offering His life and pouring out His life as a redemptive gift to the nations, it all makes sense. Now I understand how God's plan works. Being reconciled, learning the word of God, and altering my understanding into His ways has produced results. Jesus poured out His life as a gift offering, and seven thousand years later, that favour is still flowing. This phenomenon must be legitimate for us also! Having overcome our fallen nature, we also can be poured out upon the earth through the Holy Spirit. This offering will be given before the day of wrath comes - another redemptive gift of His grace to the nations.

Being conscious of the lie in the world governing humanity and watching the suffering of the people makes me look higher into God's plan. In the last days, God proclaims, *I will pour out my Spirit on all people. Your sons and daughters will prophesy, your young men will see visions, your old men will dream dreams* - Acts 2:17. God will do what is necessary for the saving of the nations. If it takes a tribulation on the earth, so they look to Him, then so be it.

The curtain between individuals' inner and outer existence needs to be free flowing to draw the Glory here on earth. *Neither height nor depth, nor anything else in all creation, will separate us from the love of God that is in Christ Jesus our Lord* - Roman 8:39. The mortal soul and flesh have been the partition between God and man. *The moment Christ 'gave up his spirit' the curtain of the temple was torn in two from top to bottom* - Matthew 27:50. This curtain is the membrane within the mortal soul - that voice telling us we are separated from Him. We are not! We are one body, one life, one will, taking part together here on earth and ready for the outpouring, which is the glorification and power of Christ upon His people. God's ultimate eradication of sin! God's righteousness will be recognised, and we will see His Glory.

Instead of being mortals burdened with a shameful nature, the Glory will shine upon those chosen. The saints will undergo a fundamental, instant transformation, *we shall all be changed, in a moment, in the twinkling of an eye* - 1 Corinthians 15:51. I believe the Glory will come upon all who have conquered their own sinful nature. Glory is heavy upon the shoulders of a sinful people. Glory is beautifying to those who have overcome. *Let your light shine before men, that they may see your good works, and glorify your Father in heaven* - Matthew 5:16.

How straight is the way and narrow the path that leads to holiness! Since death came through the window of humanity, the resurrection of the dead comes the same way. Supernatural means beyond natural! Glorification and resurrection are heavenly. Together we have the heavenly existence of God walking upon the earth in mankind. Heavenly people on earth, that's where we started before the downfall of humanity. *Do you not know that those who run in a race all run, but one receives the prize? Run in such a way that you may obtain it* - 1 Corinthians 9:24.

Years ago, the Lord directed me to give up my possessions, career, wealth to follow Him. This was a significant event, as I had my identity built in the world. Throughout time we collect communities, possessions, identities within our social structure. We may experience God and follow Him in this system. But when you step out of the world system and give up all that was valuable, that's when you understand there is a higher realm. The world declares itself as the true existence! What I have found is that the invisible realm has more honour, delight, and significance.

The toughest battle that I discovered was the theory of home. When presented without a dwelling or possessions, the thought looms large on every angle. Where is home? Your friends and family become the thorn in your side. They all say, "Are you doing something wrong?" Just as Job in the Bible lost all, and he was squatting in the dust, his friends asking him, "Are you doing something unethical?" Deep in my centre I recognised I was seeking the directions of the Lord, but I didn't perceive what He was achieving in me, it's a trust exercise. This is authentic faith, pursuing someone blindly!

About eleven years into seeking the Lord out in the wilderness, I became comfortable within myself. I didn't know where I would sleep each night, but a place would show up every day. If it didn't, I'd pitched a tent in the wilderness somewhere under a tree or beside a river. It trained me how to trust and rest upon the Lord. It also brought me to the place of appreciating that home is nowhere and everywhere. The initial thing people ask me is, where do I live? My answer always comes back as the same - nowhere but everywhere.

So, behind the security, safety, comfort, regular perception of home came honour that I was elected to sense behind what we have considered normal in our society. *Foxes have dens and birds have nests, but the Son of Man has no place to lay his head* - Luke 9:58. I realise how the Lord felt because I have walked in His shoes. To become glorified requires us to go beyond what looks natural to enter the supernatural. Supernatural, in my eyes, means faith in His power to construct a fresh creation.

Fallen humanity created our realities on earth. God created parameters for humans to live. Humans 'free will' created the mess within those parameters. To be the change that is needed, we're required to rest in the creator by faith. *Without faith it is impossible to please Him, for he who comes to God must believe that He is, and that He is a rewarder of those who diligently seek Him* - Hebrew 11:6.

Kneeling before God, I appreciate who is the creator and who has the plan. Not my will Lord but your will be done! The same words Jesus declared as the soldiers reached for Him. He identified His plight on earth was not His will - it was the Father in heaven. Getting past ourselves and appreciating who commands this story upon the earth is faith. *I am crucified with Christ: nevertheless, I live; yet not I, but Christ lives in me: and the life which I now live in the flesh I live by the faith of the Son of God, who loved me, and gave himself for me* - Galatians 2:20.

Once, as I camped in a canyon in the rain for four days, I dropped, away within myself and arrived at nothingness. God met me there! He disclosed Himself to me in the mist that had fallen in the canyon. What I stared at was God beyond my idolatry. What had become significant to me was not meaningful anymore. He says, *Have no other Gods before Me -*

Exodus 20:3-5. That scripture reached the top ten in God's list of commandments. It's part of the overcoming process. When I experienced His presence, I had no other Gods before Him, not even myself. I was in nothingness and He was there.

The original place Adam and Eve fell was the Garden of God - their home. This loss led to individuals establishing their own homes or fields. *Unless the Lord builds the house, they Labour in vain who build it* - Psalm 127:1. If you have not got the Lord building your house, your house will be insignificant. *You look for much, but behold, it comes to little; when you bring it home, I blow it away. Why? declares the Lord of hosts, because My house which lies desolate, while each of you runs to his own house* - Haggai 1:9. My house is the Lord's, and His house is our life!

Another handicap that evolved on the original people was wandering the earth. When Cain slew Abel, the Lord assigned Cain to wander the earth. I am positive most of us have a Cain in our back closet of hand-me-downs from our forefathers. *The LORD is long-suffering, and of great mercy, forgiving iniquity and transgression, and by no means clearing the guilty, visiting the iniquity of the fathers upon the sons to the third and fourth generation* - Exodus 20:5. Rebellion, wandering, murder, lies, blame was just the introductory few elements that mortals practiced on the darkened side of the road. Thus, the downward drift into debauchery advanced in every civilisation since the beginning of humanity.

Let's look at the house! I understand when God declares, "Build my house and I will establish yours," that speaks to me as we are His dwelling place. The transcript speaks, **to him who overcomes I will grant to sit with Me on My throne, as I also overcame and sat down with My Father on His throne** - Revelations 3:21.

The tabernacle of God is the life and body He has granted humans. It is a shared life not kept by us for our own pleasure.

This submitting is the overcoming process, so in the end, we will stand before the King without spot or blemish. *I beseech you therefore, brethren, by the mercies of God, that you present your bodies a living sacrifice, holy, acceptable to God, which is your reasonable service* - Romans 12:11.

We must progress through the giving-up process and become who we were appointed to become. The Lord adds, *instead of your shame you will receive a double portion, and instead of disgrace you will rejoice in your inheritance. And so, you will inherit a double portion in your land, and everlasting joy will be yours* - Isaiah 61:7.

Glorify the Lord by receiving what has been hidden in heaven. *So, your barns will be filled with plenty, and your vats will overflow with new wine* - Proverb 3:10. It is our right as followers to take up our portion. I have determined that our portion will not develop until you are standing in an overcoming position before the Lord. But the seed falling on good soil refers to someone who hears the word and understands it. *This is the one who produces a crop, yielding a hundred, sixty or thirty times what was sown* - Matthew 13:23. We go from Glory to Glory, and heaven opens as we overcome. Our portion can take place in various forms.

I don't own possessions, but my peace and quietness are a hundred-fold. I have what I need for today and I experience safety and security. My place is prepared in heaven, and eternity is waiting for me to return! Having knowledge in the Lord is abundantly more than I could hope or think. And I know I am blessed, and my family is blessed. Knowing who you are in Him gives you a rest that surpasses all understanding. Having faith and trust in Him goes beyond just knowing the Lord by name - it's having a relationship with Him. *Eye has not seen, nor ear heard, nor have entered the heart of man the things which God has prepared for those who love Him* - 1Corintians 2:9.

Conquering your world and all its trappings, you will discover God fulfilling His vows of restoration. Fulfilling a part of scripture is bringing all the tithes into His house. His house isn't just the institutionalized sanctuary; His house is the earth and all that is in it. *For all the animals of the forest are mine, and I own the cattle on a thousand hills* - Psalm 50:7-10. The tithe is your increase in your investments and the sale of your houses.

For years the institutionalized congregation has asserted transferring the tithe to them. But if you study scripture it says to bring the first fruit of your offering to them, not your tithe. I understand the tithe belongs to good works or missions that you have selected as good works. Choose carefully where you sow your seed. *The kingdom of heaven may be compared to a man who sowed good seed in his field* - Matthew 13:24.

We must adopt the field and consider the production of the soil that you are propagating. Unfortunately, there are many individuals who have evil soil but still beg for subscriptions to yield nothing except load their bags with your money.

LORD, you alone are my portion and my cup; you make my lot secure. The boundary lines have fallen for me in pleasant places; surely, I have a delightful inheritance. I will praise the LORD, who counsels me; even at night my heart instructs me. I keep my eyes always on the LORD. With him at my right hand, I will not be shaken. Therefore, my heart is glad and my tongue rejoices; my body also will rest secure, because you will not abandon me to the realm of the dead, nor will you let your faithful one see decay. You make known to me the path of life; you will fill me with joy in your presence, with eternal pleasures at your right-hand - Psalm 16:5-11.

My time with the Lord has been a drink offering poured out. This had to take place so He could fill me with new wine. New wine means promises kept by Him. *And no one pours new wine into old wineskins. Otherwise, the wine will burst the skins, and both the wine and the wineskins will be ruined. No, they pour new wine into new wineskins* Mark 2:22. Our bodies have been a living sacrifice just as we have poured our life out. *Therefore, I urge you, brothers and sisters, in view of God's mercy, to offer your bodies as a living sacrifice, holy and pleasing to God—this is your true and proper worship* - Romans 12:1. Have nothing sensual in your eyes, mind, and body that attracts you away from the Lord being first in your life. *Love the Lord your God with all your heart, and with all your soul, and with all your mind, and with all your strength, and lean not on your own understanding* - Mark 12-29:31.

To follow the Lord has been the hardest plight I have embarked upon in this life. It took everything I knew! Every thought I had and the pride I possessed needed to be humbled to receive the totality of who He is in me. Changing our lives over so the life manifests His Glory and likeness is astounding. And now, *Father, glorify me in your presence with the glory I had with you before the world began* - John 17:5.

We experience seasons in our life. There's a time to pull down and a time to rise back up again. Once we have gone through the fires of God and emptied ourselves of all items that were before the Father as idols, then He will restore us into His appointed destiny. Before that time, we would have boasted of ourselves. We will recognise the Glory of the Lord on the earth in and through the person of God who has overcome.

I walk in the way of righteousness, along the paths of justice, bestowing wealth on those who love me and making their treasuries full - Proverbs 8:21. It is imperative that we, as a Holy people a chosen race, are seen by Him standing in faith in the coming days when He returns. The women who had oil in their lamps were taken with the Lord, oil represents faith.

I tell you, He will give justice to them speedily. Nevertheless, when the Son of Man comes, will He find faith on earth? - Luke 18:8.

I have had a problem in my life of being a bull at a gate. It means I have tunnel vision and continue advancing until one of two things takes place. The gate opens, and it gives me great strength because there is a big lesson behind the gate, or the gate remains shut. Throughout my walk on this path of Holiness, God has taught me to be still and know He is Lord and this requires the gift of Grace! Grace is the function to remain in stillness. Stillness is where Grace can enter with power so we can receive. If we could push the gates open by our strength, it would fill our pride. And pride got us into this position at the collapse of humanity in the Garden of God.

Another spot within our lives that keeps us apart from the gifts and favour of God is a spirit called the 'Baron Woman'. This spirit places us before God in pride. It also puts God into our convenience and timing instead of putting us into God's convenience. We are one with God, but we can't put Him into our timing or convenience. This one thing will cause the windows of heaven to remain shut over our heads.

But He said to me, "My grace is sufficient for you, for my power is made perfect in weakness." Therefore, I will boast all the more gladly about my weaknesses, so that Christ's power may rest on me - 2 Corinthians 12:9.

If you follow the Lord with your whole heart, He will take you beyond yourself, talents, ability, and possessions. He will find your weaknesses and bring them to the surface so He can be strong and give us victory.

Gideon had an army of ten thousand going into battle against around thirty-four thousand. He declared that if any of you are afraid, leave now. Twice repeating the same request, all but three hundred soldiers left. This left Gideon to fight a battle with the Lord, plus three hundred. The Lord gave Gideon the victory because he didn't keep the surrounding weakness - he only fought with strength.

That's what our walk into Grace on the path of holiness is - releasing our weaknesses and taking hold of His strength. The Lord God has stripped me of houses, possessions, fears, all to make me strong. Resting in Him, I know *His Grace is sufficient* and a place of great strength. As He's restored me, I know not to boast in my ability because I know from where it came. *The Lord is gracious to whom He is gracious to and merciful to whom he is merciful to* - Exodus 33:18. His Word says we go from Glory to Glory - this is how it happens through our weaknesses to His strength.

We need to rise up into our proper position in the Kingdom of God. He will declare, *come up here, and I will show you what must take place after this* - Revelation 4:1. It won't be because we have a great prayer life. It will be because we overcame through the Blood of the Lamb of Our Lord Jesus Christ.

Chapter 3

Kingdom Glory

Let's sum up following the Glory of God. Originally Grace arrives, which had us saved. That's the revelation moment where Grace disturbs and inspires in the one moment. I call it the "Ah" moment when I knew God existed. Suddenly another decision became apparent to follow Him and His ways, which this took many years. Learning how He thinks and trading my thinking for His! **Take captive every thought and bring it into submission to the will of God** - 1 Corinthians 10:5. I wrote a book at this point called 'How I Overcame My Own Life'.

Then came the healing that I required. This healing is because the worldly processes, my hereditary upbringing, and the culture were flawed which made me flawed. Understanding how the spiritual world works is a big process that keeps emerging as we continue with our relationship with the Lord.

Another anointing of Grace came to me for the overcoming process - this moved me into the transference and restoration of my body and soul. The process took perseverance, endurance, and long-suffering. Remember, *His grace is sufficient*, which means it's His power and His might that cause us to emerge out of the overcoming season victorious. All He needs from us is faithfulness and obedience. Every time we move into a new facet of God, He anoints us with more Grace, which brings us to more Glory. I can always tell when He wants me to move. The Grace moves from me; that's a sure sign. Then a fresh anointing comes with the next season.

There has been so much darkness, also identified as demons, stopping the way of seeing the Glory of God. It is prayers that keep rising into the heavens that show us the way. Scripture declares, *Lift up your heads, O you gates! Lift up, you everlasting doors! And the King of glory shall come in* - Psalm 24:9.

We are the gates, and we are to clear the highway for the King to come. It's always been about Him and His Glory - it's never been about us. We can use all things when we are not feeding ourselves to advance and establish our house. Knowing who we are for His purpose and His plan, and His Kingdom.

Those rocks He speaks about are our thoughts. They have established themselves in our lives, and we fall short of the Glory. Our thoughts sit like rocks on the path or highway, and we can't see what is on the other side. They hinder us from our future.

I learnt the power of spiritual warfare at this point. A mighty prayer is what we identify as warfare. It has authority to break rocks and move mountains. *I tell you, if you have faith as small as a mustard seed, you can say to this mountain, 'Move from here to there,' and it will move. Nothing will be impossible for you* - Matthew 17:20. This power lives within faith, and that same faith lives in you.

Before we came to earth, we were living with God in another atmosphere. We can't look back because it was before time was. Our purpose and plan are written in the book of life and imprinted on our DNA. Our effort is needed to reveal what is preventing or stopping all that's been appointed from His plan from entering reality. When the Israelites crossed the desert, only three got into the Promise Land. This is because they grumbled about how God was unfair towards them and because they disputed the leadership, which was Moses and Aaron. If God appoints government leaders, it's because He needs that person to fulfil scripture. *For unto us a Child is born, unto us a Son is given; and the government shall be upon His shoulder. And His name shall be called Wonderful, Counsellor, The Mighty God, The Everlasting Father, The Prince of Peace* - Isaiah 9:6.

During the reign of President Donald Trump, I heard nothing but grumbling about his leadership. Look at what he did achieve! He got the peace treaty signed between Palestine and Israel. No other President has ever accomplished such a task. It is written in the book of Revelation as the key that starts the end time tribulation for the earth. Then when the next president came along, Joe Biden, more grumbling occurred. God chose both men. The government rests on God's shoulders, not ours. Our instruction from Him is to *pray for kings and all who are in authority so that we can live peaceful and quiet lives marked by godliness and dignity* - 1 Timothy 2:2.

God wants to break down our lives and reveal His Glory through the life He has given us on earth. The resurrection of the person and power of Jesus Christ living in and through us. Together as one! *Let the eyes of your understanding be enlightened; that you may know what is the hope of His calling, what are the riches of the glory of His inheritance in the saints* - Ephesians 1:18. This world is waiting for the manifestation of the Glory of God. *Nations will come to your light, and kings to the brightness of your dawn* - Isaiah 60:3.

The individuals who will bring His Glory are those who wash their robes. For many years the institutional religious church has called itself the body of Christ. But if this is correct, what becomes of the people who have been set aside as His special people? We were drawn out of the establishment called the church and hidden under His wing as His own special possession. *But you are a chosen people, a royal priesthood, a holy nation, God's special possession, that you may declare the praises of him who called you out of darkness into his wonderful light* - 1 Peter 2:9. He was never seeking a person who just did the routine of church and what looks good to others on the outside. He was after people who had their hearts following Him. Who would give all that they had for His purpose and His plan.

I happen to be one of those people! What a privilege to not only serve the living God but to be friends with the living God. To know His secrets for His world and to be a carrier of these secrets. Willing people becoming conduits for His Glory. The hope of His calling, "Born for Holiness". He wants to reveal His Son in us. It's been a long challenging journey for those who have overcome to follow the lamb of God. But the calling was greater than the pain. I now stand on the threshold of this hope; every fibre of my being reaches for His Glory. *And the Spirit and the bride say, "Come!" And let him who hears say, "Come!" And let him who thirsts come. Whoever desires, let him take the water of life freely* - Revelation 22:17.

When man landed on the moon, we, the people, came together, all fixated on the landing. Every eye in every nation was focused on this great day for mankind. That was man's finest achievement as one tribe coming together simultaneously. If that's man's best achievement, we are running short! I looked at one of God's accomplishments, and He filled the earth with trees, night, day, waters, animals, man, and woman all in six days.

In comparison, man can't do anything without God. It was God who gave us that incredible success, and the men in that moon craft knew it. They all gave God thanks! When the Son of God comes back, we will have another defining moment in time that will change everything. *Behold, He is coming with clouds, and every eye will see Him, even they who pierced Him. And all the tribes of the earth will mourn because of Him* - Revelation 1:7. It's Christ's return that will cause mankind to look in one direction. *For it is written, as I live, saith the Lord, every knee shall bow to Me, and every tongue shall confess to God* - Romans 14:11. He has prepared His elect, called the Bride, for His Glory.

In this present time, we who are prepared will be used to set the captives free from wickedness. *And it shall come to pass afterward, that I will pour out my spirit upon all flesh; and your sons and your daughters shall prophesy, your old men shall dream dreams, your young men shall see visions* - Joel 2:28. We need to move our focus from man's achievements into what God can do. We stand on the brink of this Glory being realised on earth. A defining moment for all of mankind! But it won't be *by my might nor by my power, but by My Spirit, says the LORD of Hosts* - Zachariah 4:6.

Lift up your heads, you gates; lift them up, you ancient doors, that the King of glory may come in - Psalm 24:9. This scripture means clear the path of all thoughts that are opposed to the God of all creation coming into your life and world. Our attention needs to be realigned to His plan, not our own.

Another obscurity to be recognised is a darkness that withholds any good thing from us. *For the Lord God is a sun and shield: The Lord will give Grace and Glory: no good thing will He withhold from them that walk uprightly* - Psalm 84:11. I have been positioned in faith, ready to pick up the inheritance God portioned for me. *LORD, you alone are my portion and my cup; you make my lot secure* - Psalm 16:5. Many demons block that day from happening.

Restrictions were around me, withholding the promises of God. It is up to us to recognise the antichrist within our minds. Taking back what was stolen throughout the generations, we will encounter opposition. Going forward in the soul and restoring all that belongs to the King, we will see His Kingdom established on earth. It is time to shine! *I will go before you and level the exalted places, I will break in pieces the doors of bronze and cut through the bars of iron* - Isaiah 45:2. We have been busy telling our story! But it is time to reveal God's story and take back what belongs to us.

I have heard preachers preach about the end times of this world. But most of those perceptions have been short-sighted. Something didn't add up to the story of God. Man's explanation had us leaving earth before the tribulation, but this is not true according to the scriptures. There will be a great horde of people come out of this End Time period upon the earth who have washed their robes and standing with Our Lord Jesus Christ in their hearts. But we'll see **that in the last days there will come times of difficulty. For people will be lovers of self, lovers of money, proud, arrogant, abusive, disobedient to their parents, ungrateful, unholy, heartless, unappeasable, slanderous, without self-control, brutal, not loving good, treacherous, reckless, swollen with conceit, lovers of pleasure rather than lovers of God, having the appearance of godliness, but denying its power. Avoid such people** - 2 Timothy 3: 1-5.

If the preachers were right about the gathering together in the air of the saints, and we all get taken away, it would leave the earth void of the presence of God through these dark times. I believe God is to use these people for the establishment of the Kingdom of God on the earth.

Dear fellow believers,

For years you have called yourself the 'Church'. That thought implied we the people had to be and stand in the congregation to be called 'The Body of Christ'.

That is not the truth!

The Body of Christ comprises the truck drivers, the protestors and the freedom fighters. The voice against the dictatorship of this nation and world at the moment! You, however, are the power behind these people because this is your body. Your prayers back these brave fighters and the blood of Christ will cover them in the battle that is emerging. Many, in the coming days, will lose their life for the freedoms they are standing for. Use what we have been given - PRAYER!

Then they will deliver you over to be persecuted and killed, and you will be hated by all nations because of My name. **At that time many will fall away** *-* Matthew 24:9. These people will be persecuted in these coming days. See them as the 'Body of Christ' because they are!

I've had freedom fighters who have never stood in a church but believe in their heart that Jesus is their Lord come to me asking for PRAYER. They come back every few days for PRAYER because they feel protected once I pray. Their knees are bowing as I speak.

I don't send these people into a church because I am 'The Church' and you are the church. It was never the building!

He who finds his life will lose it, and he who loses his life for My sake will find it - Matthew 10:39.

Letting go of your life as you know it is difficult. I know I did it. But I discovered my life in Him, the one who created me. I found home, purpose, meaning, future, and treasures beyond what man could offer as riches. It was like holding the keys to heaven and hell and overcoming the hell attached to the keys to living with heaven upon the earth. The keys to heaven and hell live within us because they lived with Our Lord Jesus Christ.

Identifying the living God is beyond what I could hope for or think. Individuals can believe in God. But to experience Him is another step. Intimacy only comes from spending time with God and hearing and being in His presence. Wanting to know Him means having nothing before your eyes except God Himself and His plans. *Then you shall see and become radiant, and your heart shall swell with joy; Because the abundance of the sea shall be turned to you, the wealth of the Gentiles shall come to you* - Isaiah 60:5. *Nations will come to your light, and kings to the brightness of your dawn* - Isaiah 60.

To walk in purity, we will face many demons on our path to holiness. Another division from God is our thinking, which can sear our subconscious closed. It causes even the elect of God, if possible, to be deceived. *For false Christs and false prophets will arise and will show great signs and wonders, to mislead, if possible, even the elect* - Matthew 24:24. I have met the elect of God who carry Christ's spirit in the centre of their being. But they still have pockets of thinking that are out of order. *That they all may be one, as You, Father, are in Me, and I in You; that they also may be one in Us, that the world may believe that You sent Me* - John 17:21.

These pockets of thinking in the elect of God can separate them from all the Father has for them. It is very difficult for them to see their own thinking separating them because their subconscious has been seared shut. These people have a slight arrogance of pride still within their being because they know who they are, 'the elect'. They think they have all aspects covered, and nobody can tell them differently. They call themselves prophets of God, but if they bring thinking from universal thinking or any other space other than God's Word, they are deceiving people and themselves. The elect can use the Word of God in the wrong context and this is also deceiving others and themselves. Wrong terminology out of God's order of timing is also a deception. Be aware of what is around us and whom we are listening to. *Be alert and of sober mind. Your enemy the devil prowls around like a roaring lion looking for someone to devour* - 1 Peter 5:8. If the devil can get you to believe any lies, we haven't reached the perfection of holiness.

Jesus Christ's walk on earth was all about the Kingdom of God. This earthy walk was to open our eyes of our understanding to show us His Father's Kingdom and love. His Kingdom was the message! What does that Kingdom look like beyond our own understanding? It carries the power and authority over all that is on the earth today. But more than that, it is up to us to subdue the earth, so His Kingdom becomes the reigning Kingdom.

Today we recognise we are having many troubles with the governing authorities over the earth. God's people who carry the Kingdom of God within their being will replace these authorities, but not yet; the time hasn't come before the end. God gave Adam and Eve the Garden of Eden. He told them to have dominion and subdue the earth. Subdue means to overcome, quieten or bring under control. The earth belongs to the King, Our Lord Jesus Christ. It's our job as the body of Christ to take this Kingdom back and present it to the King for His reign on earth. He will give the saints authority to rule with Our Lord Jesus Christ for a thousand years upon the earth. I have written much more about this subject later in this book.

While this transaction is taking place, God breaks down what we have called Daniel's prophecy of the ages. The head of the body that He describes in the book of Daniel is gold. The arms and chest are silver. The belly and thighs are brass. The last two stages are where the legs of iron and the feet of clay are mixed but are being broken down. These descriptions are the ages we have lived through. Iron and clay are our time now. The End Times! But even this is divided by the time of sorrow and the Tribulation. These end-time days last seven years, according to the book of Daniel. During this time the Kingdom of God will be established as the kingdom of darkness is coming to the totality upon the earth and a finish.

The Abomination of the desolation or the Son of perdition will show himself as leader of all the earth. Who is this leader? I can only speculate about this answer! Since 1920 a group called the 'One World Government' has been putting their plan together to control humankind. This plan has what the Bible calls a mark of the beast. In recent days I understand this as the vaccination that people are being forced to have. They are claiming we can't travel, buy or sell or cross over borders unless we have this vaccination. Within the vaccination is a genetic DNA modifier. It transforms your own DNA, and it can't change back to your original origin. This product mRNA is patented, according to an authority, which could be correct but may not be correct, and it's up to us to check out details. This product appears under the heading of Trans-Human which means you belong to the people who keep the patent. It doesn't bring you under the Human Rights act anymore. So, if you require prosecuting for sicknesses this product has brought on, you can't. Because in the eyes of the law, you are Trans- Human! It's something out of a science fiction flick. But in reality, so is God and His plan!

This is the great falling away or separation of the goat and the sheep or the breakdown of clay and iron as it has been interpreted.

Who is the leader? He hasn't been revealed yet! He is there waiting his time to stand in the Abomination of the Desolation. I picture the abomination of the desolation as a man claiming he is God where God would stand.

As this separation is happening, it will become more and more obvious who is serving darkness and who is serving the light of God. But then we will see great persecution, and many will fall away from the faith.

God's likeness will appear with Glory upon those who have been washed. And His righteousness will be seen upon them. *See, darkness covers the earth and thick darkness is over the peoples, but the LORD rises upon you and his glory appears over you. Nations will come to your light, and kings to the brightness of your dawn* - Isaiah 60:1.

The individuals who have made themselves ready to usher the Kingdom of God into the earth have been bought at a price. They have been humbled to receive all that the King of Glory has for them to display on the earth. Any gift from God comes from Grace! Through faith, praise and thanksgiving releases the power, goodness, kindness, and generosity of His blessings into the life you have called your own. Then we can boast in Him how great is our God! His righteousness will be seen over those who conquered their own behaviour to follow Him and His ways.

Every day I remain on earth, I become more aware of how limited I know the Lord. It's going to take an eternity to delve into all the facets of His wondrous worlds and to know Him intimately. To know Him is to love Him. To be humbled by Him shows me how far I have to go to *be perfect, as your Father which is in heaven is perfect* - Matthew 5:48.

Prosperity among God's people has been a complex subject because some have preached differently than what I understood it to be. God told the rich man to sell all and give it to the poor. *Yet He says, the wealth of the wicked is laid up for the righteous* - Proverbs 13:22.

To become righteous is the walk of prosperity, not the possessions of the world. To have no separation between the Kingdom of God and ourselves is righteousness.

Often, I pray the prayers that you would think would move heaven. But in fact, they push me into alignment with the Kingdom of God. So, the separation is taken out of me. There is just one Kingdom, not two, and my thinking opposed the Kingdom.

Once this alignment has happened, we walk in unity with the Holy Spirit with one voice and one movement. The rich man didn't have the Kingdom of God as His focus; he had his riches. The righteous see their life as His who bought them at a price. *He is the one who will build a house for my name. And I will secure his royal throne forever* - 2 Samuel 7:13. His house is our house, which is our bodies and life as a living temple.

To go beyond our own selves is the art of life. I have been diligent in this process for twenty-six years, but still, I find separations that need to be removed.

Renewing our mind is part of the separation and *casting down imaginations, and every high thing that exalted itself against the knowledge of God, and bringing into captivity every thought to the obedience of Christ* - 2 Corinthians 10:5.

When we humbly walk with the Holy Spirit, knowing He knows all things, that's when we partner with the purposes of the Kingdom coming into the earth. Separating the Holy Spirit from ourselves and stepping in front of Him, causes us not to receive the promises. *I am the vine, you are the branches. He who abides in Me, and I in him, bears much fruit; for without Me you can do nothing* - John 15:5. I don't know how many times in life I have stepped in front of the Holy Spirit, but it has produced the same result - not receiving promises!

Every time a task is given from the Lord, make sure it's His Glory that will be seen, not yours. *I am the LORD: that is my name: and my glory will I not give to another* - Isaiah 42:8. This is where we shall see no separation between God and His followers. When He declares to build His house, and He will build our house, my interpretation is that means we are in one accord, working for the same house and dwelling together. *And, behold, I come quickly; and my reward is with me, to give every man according to his work* - Revelation 22:12. To build upon the foundations of Our Lord Jesus Christ and to do the Father's work is our work. *Then Jesus answered and said to them, most assuredly, I say to you, the Son can do nothing of Himself, but what He sees the Father do; for whatever He does, the Son also does in like manner* - John 5:19.

Following the path of righteousness and holiness will lead us into the purpose and promises of God. It's like coming to the end of yourself to step into His Glory, accompanied by the Father, Son, and the Holy Spirit. Following God's step, we will fulfil our purpose or mission upon the earth.

Halleluiah

A supernatural collaboration of people coming simultaneously together for the greater good of humanity is 'Thy Kingdom Come'. *And when the day of Pentecost was fully come, they were all with one accord in one place* - Act 2:1.

When we can't be disillusioned by the world and its opportunities anymore, is when we are looking into the eyes of our creator ready for this new coming. It's been a timing thing between people and God. Only those who have prepared themselves will be ready to receive. But it is still up to us to step out onto the wings of the High and Mighty God, and together we shall run towards the goal.

Imagine the reversing of all the disappointments, loss of opportunities, love, and possessions! We would see the curse reversed and stand in the Kingdom's moment. It takes a lot of overcoming to get to the spot of just being in the day at the moment, not wanting anything. Enjoying the passing of the day with all the gifts on that day. I have chased God to the end of the earth to be where I stand today in Him with peace and to have the quietness of mind. I have perfected a vision on paper that He gave me twenty-six years ago but it is still in paper form; it hasn't come alive upon the earth. I can't bring that vision to life - it needs to be from the realm of the supernatural, otherwise it's my strength and my power.

Most of humanity speaks from their understanding. Moving from our knowledge and words into His presence will project His Glory and righteousness upon the earth. *The Gentiles shall see your righteousness, and all kings your glory. You shall be called by a new name, which the mouth of the LORD will name* - Isaiah 62:2.

He says, *not by might nor by power, but by My Spirit, saith the Lord of hosts* - Zechariah 4:6. He disables our power and might to enable His power and His might. This disabling takes us out of ourselves to stand on the same ground as Him in His garden upon His earth. Nothing belongs to us, *for all the animals of the forest are mine, and I own the cattle on a thousand hills. I know every bird on the mountains, and all the animals in the field are mine. If I were hungry, I would not tell you, for all the world is mine and everything in it* - Psalm 50 10-12.

We may all do life differently and have different visions, different living quarters, and different plans, but when all is said and done, we own nothing. We came into this world with nothing, and we will leave with nothing. The one true Judge will weigh all things done and said upon the earth. *For we must all appear before the judgment seat of Christ; that every one may receive the things done in his body, according to that he has done, whether it be good or bad* - 2 Corinthians 5:12.

Beyond our interpretation of life is God's interpretation of His Kingdom. When we come to the end of our might and power and know who the King and Lord is all can come under Grace, and we can call this success. The world's success differs completely from God's success.

The world asks, how much have you accumulated in the bank? Do you own your own house? How much super have you gained? What is your plan for the next ten years?

God says *to him who overcomes I will grant to sit with Me on My throne, as I also overcame and sat down with My Father on His throne* - Revelations 3:21.

For where your treasure is, there your heart will be also - Matthew 6:21. If your heart is in the world, that's where your treasure is. If your heart is with God and His Kingdom coming to the earth, that's where your treasure is. Distinct opposite outcomes and perceptions! One finishes when you die; the other carries heavenly ramifications. The Judgement Seat of Christ judges both at the end.

Overcoming the calamities of our mind and the works of our hands, we will enter the rest of God. Six days God laboured, but on the seventh He rested. He created the rest day for man. *Here remains a Sabbath-rest for the people of God; for anyone who enters God's rest also rests from their works, just as God did from His* - Hebrew 4:9-10.

All of us have our portion in life! We're born into a family, a culture, a town, and country. All of us have to make our way back home to the Father's Garden. Love, Faith, Hope are the elements we follow. The face of Christ and His image is the perfection we look for. The threshold we will cross only when we have conquered the world, our works, and ourselves. Sovereignty over one's self that's called liberty. People look to the world and governments to find liberty or sovereignty but they will never find it until they focus on the one who is free who has no dimensions limiting Him. The Almighty God!

We have been born onto the earth in a body that's confinement within a dimension of this reality. The body will wither and die! *For what is your life? It is even a vapor that appears for a little time and then vanishes away* - James 4:14. We can experience being with the Lord here on earth in the body if we seek His presence beyond our knowledge and words. I've had many encounters with His presence, too many to mention in this book. But we can go further than just having encounters. We can see Him every day in the life you have called your own. Moving into His presence will bring a new intimacy and an array of Him to the earth. Count your blessings in a day they will overtake you. *Every good gift and every perfect gift are from above, coming down from the Father of lights with whom there is no variation or shadow due to change* - James 1:17.

If you've looked at the glass half full, start seeing it full and overflowing. **My cup runs over** - Psalm 23:5.

Time is too precious to waste on meditations of the world and its calamities. Open your eyes to see more of Him everywhere in your day. Give thanks for the gifts in today. Ask for new horizons to open up before you. Yesterday is gone. Open unto me the opportunity of why you sent me to earth. *Being confident of this very thing, that He who has begun a good work in you will complete it until the day of Jesus Christ* - Philippians 1:6.

When the desire birthed within your life is operating in a healed manner, it will signal you to complete the original task you were placed on the earth to accomplish. This call will beckon your horizons beyond where you have been in your past. Dreams are a narrative of desires; they dictate to us the direction we should take. Desires are the call to live beyond today. They call us to attention and action. When you're in your calling, you will feel the joy of your heart coming alive and awakening to the day as you throb with joy. Then, wonder will be revived, and the essence will permeate from your body as you breathe.

I have kept the path of overcoming and given up my ways of thinking for a new way. This thinking has come from God the Father! Not from another human or group. It has taken many years, but these years of giving up all that I had become so I could be who He called me to be will be renewed.

Once you have crossed over the threshold of your mind, you will enter a new place of being. The heart is healed, your mind renewed, and we will feel the connection with love. Love has always been there, but when you're in conflict with love, you can't feel the entire expanse of love's presence. It's also a new place of receiving beyond any other place I have been. *Above all, love each other, because love covers over a multitude of sins -* 1 Peter 4.

I just had an encounter with being so loved by my family that it felt alien to the life I had been living. I was spoilt, nourished, and made so comfortable - I thought I would settle into this comfort and never leave. Instead, I left their house to walk into another house full of love, comfort, food, and conversation. This love was always there but I couldn't feel the full effects, because I was still in the separation of love and home within myself.

Reaching this place where the separation from one's self has been closed, it feels like all the limitations have been lifted off and you 're standing in infinity. We need to find this love in ourselves for ourselves. Many people look for a home and love outside themselves. But if they would start from the inside and intergrade home and love into themselves, they would have a different result. Once this separation is completed, we will be ready for the true self to surface into the world to complete the task given to us by the creator before time was.

Love was always the bottom line of life. To renew our mind, which is our world, and move into our heart, which is love, it will give a different result. *Love never fails. But whether there are prophecies, they will fail; whether there are tongues, they will cease; whether there is knowledge, it will vanish away* - 1 Corinthians 13:8. Love carries us, *but they who wait for the Lord shall renew their strength: they shall mount up with wings like eagles; they shall run and not be weary; they shall walk and not faint* - Isaiah 40:31. The love that is not separated from one's self will be enough to complete the life you have called your own. Anything else will take us outside ourselves, and that is like chasing the wind.

I now look at my friends in a new light because I'm a friend to myself. Before I crossed the threshold of love, I was still seeking to overcome my world and self. It had me separated from being a loving friend to others. We need to love ourselves with the same love we give to others. *Love the Lord your God with all your heart and with all your soul and with all your mind and with all your strength. The second is this: 'Love your neighbour as yourself. 'There is no commandment greater than these'* - Mark 12:30:31.

Any romance needs to go deeper and deeper to enjoy the freshness of the newness in each other. The same goes with the relationship we have with the Lord. My walk into Holiness had me meet Him in my belief system within myself. I then had to agree to follow Him and His ways. This had me overcome my thinking and habits, which healed my body and soul of spiritual abuse. The devil can only get to us if we have these breaches within our soul exposed or still open to the darkness. Once the breaches are closed within the soul, peace returns to the person who has been diligent to follow the thinking and ways of God. A new prayer arises within asking for this freshness of the relationship to emerge. *Come near to God and He will come near to you. Wash your hands, you sinners, and purify your hearts, you double-minded* - James 4:8.

God is like a diamond! He moves slightly, and light emulates from the facets of His being. This light is new horizons, fresh encounters, or revelations of who He is or what He wants upon the earth. *If his son asks for bread, will He give him a stone?* - Matthew 7:9. If we ask, we will receive fresh revelations, directions of His plan from the book of life.

To recap, living upon the earth in stages is fascinating. In youth, we have adventure, we proceed to the responsibility of raising a family and working in the desired field of expertise. From that era, we shift into rediscovering who we are because we seem to be lost in who we became and the titles we gained along the way. Once we're through the rediscovery of self-process comes enjoyments of being a grandparent. This process has time to be still in every moment and appreciate the innocence of life. Through some processes, it's hard to enjoy life when you're working hard to supply and raise a family. It's hard to enjoy when you're rediscovering who you are in life. But it's easy to enjoy life when you have arrived at just being who you were made to be without struggling to do, be or find the reasons why. *So, I concluded there is nothing better than to be happy and enjoy ourselves as long as we can. And people should eat and drink and enjoy the fruits of their labour, for these are gifts from God* - Ecclesiastes 3:12-13.

I look at others of my age group in their 60s, and they have set themselves up in houses, superannuation, and a hobby or two to keep them interested in life. My life has no house I own, no rental house I live in, no savings in the bank, and only enough belongings to fit into a sports car. I did this because, *Jesus said to them, the one who has left home or wife or brothers or parents or children for the sake of the kingdom of God will receive many times as much in this age and, in the age to come, eternal life* - Luke 18:29.

The life I have chosen is beyond what society claims is normal. Careers, houses, savings, and hobbies these things will not fulfil the individual. I'm only realizing now that every moment is precious, and every moment has life. *The thief comes to steal, to kill, and to destroy. I have come that they may have life, and that they may have it* **more abundantly** - John 10:10. So, in other words, we can sit in our comforts of what we have achieved but miss what God has in His plan. *Enter through the narrow gate. For wide is the gate and broad is the road that leads to destruction, and many enter through it* - Matthew 7:13. The wide gate can focus us on the wrong things and we never accomplish what we were put upon the earth to achieve. It's easy to lose that focus if you see everybody else around you owning what the world has instructed people to possess, but their ownership becomes their prison. Remember that righteousness and glory in the Lord was the goal for humanity, not how much we own. *For behold, darkness shall cover the earth, and deep darkness the people; But the LORD will arise over you, And His glory will be seen upon you* - Isaiah 60:2.

But you are **a chosen generation, a royal priesthood, a** *Holy nation, His own special people, that you may proclaim the praises of Him who called you out of darkness into His marvellous light* - 1Peter 2:9. Knowing your destiny beyond what the world offers is higher than accumulating the wealth in this lifetime. *For where your treasure is, there your heart will be also* - Matthew 6:21.

Chapter 4

Beyond the Veil

In this next part of the journey, our foot has not stepped upon the ground, nor has our eyes seen. We will move beyond our own understanding. Once the appetites of the world are behind us, we can walk through the veil of the unknown, being dead to the world and all it offers.

But as it is written, eye has not seen, nor ear heard, neither have entered into the heart of man, the things which God has prepared for them that love him - 1 Corinthians 2:9.

God warned Lot and his family not to turn around when they were fleeing Sodom and Gomorrah. Lot's wife swung around and turned into salt. This is the same reason we're required to look forward and not backward on this divine journey. *You are the salt of the earth, but if the salt has lost its flavour, with what will it be salted? It is then good for nothing, but to be cast out and trodden under the feet of men* - Matthew 5:13. Glancing back into the world will stop you from progressing into what you haven't seen.

In this fresh season of intimacy with the Lord, we will encounter Him coming to us through the veil. He came to us first! But it has been up to us to follow Him and His ways. He satisfied all our needs and now it's our position to rest in His presence. Our heart cries out for a fresh encounter of intimacy. And the porthole of prayer opens up the way for Him to come. *The voice of one crying in the wilderness: Prepare the way of the LORD; Make straight in the desert a highway for our God -* Isaiah 40:3.

Sadly, we may still have an orphan spirit attached to our hopes, and that may stop the fullness of this new intimacy behind the veil, with the Lord emerging. Along the way, we have been disappointed and let down, and this creates the orphan spirit. Orphans are regularly let down and disillusioned. They never feel the faith of having something remarkable materialize into existence. Recognising this spirit in our thoughts is the key to abolishing it from our lives. When you think back into the Garden of God, Adam and Eve would have felt this spirit in their lives once they were banished from the Garden to live outside. Hope was reduced; they felt abandoned! But requesting God to restore our oneness with Him will reinstate all things that seem to be lost. But, nothing is ever lost - it is just waiting for you to call it into recovery.

In my walk with God I have felt the pain of overcoming my weaknesses to return to the Garden within. We have forgotten how we should live because we have never experienced the fullness of what we had before the fall of humanity. Adam and Eve lived in peace within their soul. There was nothing outrageous happening that would fear them out of this place, no dramas. What I have noticed about my walk back to the Garden, the closer I get to peace, quiet, and rest between God and myself, the less I look for something to do. We are brought up to do something all the time; it is harder to just *be still, and know that I am God: I will be exalted among the heathen, I will be exalted in the earth* - Psalm 46:10. This is another place we may see the devil toiling with our thoughts, our doing instead of being. God will be exalted in His time!

I believe we need to pray, "Remind me Lord of how to live when I was whole with you in the Garden."

Walking into the throne room of the King, we wouldn't say to Him, "I want." We would ask Him what He required. We can have dreams and visions but do those dreams and visions line up with God's desires? It's better to walk into the throne room and say, "Lord, what is your desire for this life upon the earth?" It's a change of perspective! One way of asking is in humility, the other is a demand of wanting. *Fear the LORD, you his saints: for there is* **no want to them that fear him** - Psalm 34:9. This type of humility brings us next to God to reign and rule with Him. *If we endure, we shall also reign with Him. If we deny Him, He also will deny us* - 2 Timothy 2:12. Humility produces an atmosphere of being in charge instead of the atmosphere in charge of us.

Remember, Satan is the prince of the airwaves. These airwaves are our atmosphere! Our mind invites the atmosphere to be Holy or demonic. The choice of free will lives on our bottom line, along with love. Free will is only free when it's in His will. Outside of that is rebellion!

God sits outside of time - He is eternal, *declaring the end from the beginning, and from ancient times things which have not been done, saying, My plan will be established, and I will accomplish all My good pleasure* - Isaiah 46:10. If you are in a helicopter viewing a parade upon the ground, you would see the beginning from the end. God calls the beginning from the end! He has written the Bible through the Holy Spirit within individuals so we can understand what He has predicted. From Genesis through to Revelation, the story is the same. The redemption of man! Nobody can change what is written and no prayer can interrupt what is coming.

And if any man shall take away from the words of the book of this prophecy, God shall take away his part out of the book of life, and out of the Holy city, and from the things which are written in this book - Revelation 22:19.

The organised religious congregations have thinned down the Word of God. Few speak of the End Times! They like to keep their messages fluffy to not put people off the truth. They became a place to get certificates for preachers, chaplaincy, etc. When Jesus Christ released the disciples He just sent them out into the world to preach. There wasn't a certificate needed nor an organisation backing them; they just went.

We are living in a society where money is made from a course so they exploit education and certificates in all fields. Back in my day, we just went out and did what we wanted to do. We didn't need a certificate or anybody's permission; they called it taking initiative!

Once I started a motel complex for homeless men. When I arrived in the town, the resident preachers asked, "Who is covering you?" Meaning what church do I belong to! I told them that Jesus Christ was my covering, and I did not need permission from a church. I only needed God to lead and cover me. This was alien to them! But they came alongside me and helped with the men. Soon, the preachers gathered together to take the place away from me because they wanted a ministry such as I had. God didn't allow them to take over. He was in charge, not them!

God is after the heart of man, not the works of man. Thinking you're in a safe spot because you're a preacher or minister, you need to check on God's criteria for escaping the things that will come upon the earth. *Watch therefore, and pray always that you may be counted worthy to escape all these things that will come to pass, and to stand before the Son of Man* - Luke 21:36.

For years I have searched for God like gold. *If you seek her as silver, and search for her as for hidden treasures* - **Proverb 2:4. He is speaking about wisdom in that text. For me, I was searching for a stronger portrayal of myself because I recognised He lived in me.** *On that day you will know that I am in My Father, and you are in Me, and I am in you* - **John 14:20. This seeking did not fulfil me, but it was causing a better person to emerge. Beyond the works of my own hands, I came into,** *be still, and know that I am God* - **Psalm 46:10. Being still in God, I understood that all is perfect, and love lives in me. The unity of God was always there! It was I who breached this deposit of excellence because my prospects of thought and desires were impure.**

The Characteristic of love is humility. The path of holiness is not complicated, but to declare it is easy is not true. Many souls have found Jesus Christ but have not followed Him because the path of humility is challenging. Many have halted along the way and made themselves comfortable in their caves or houses. The path of holiness is the path of love; they are the same. Our centre of our being is love.

I have never detected another individual who could accept the love that my heart could lavish upon them. The only heart that can receive and give I have found is Jesus Christ Himself. We are His impression for the people we come in contact with. This reflection or impression is love. It is vital to pursue the place of humility. If we look for exalted places, they are occupied with arrogance or pride. These two features are why humanity is in the dilemma that we're seeing. In our humility, He raises us up, and *my God will meet all your needs according to the riches of his glory in Christ Jesus* - Philippians 4:19.

Many individuals study problems or systems from the level of the difficulty or the narrative of the world. Shifting your perspective to align with Jesus Christ or God the Father, you will discover all is well. The present world reads like it is in a bit of a pickle, but from where I rest watching from God's view, He is fulfilling His own scripture. *I have told you these things, so that in me you may have peace. In this world, you will have trouble. But take heart! I have overcome the world* - John 16:33. All individuals have been called to overcome the world and all its trappings. *For many are called, but few are chosen* - Matthew 22:14.

You may suppose you can escape the events that must take place, but according to scripture, you won't. We are to have peace in our minds and assurance of His plan being worked out upon the earth. Remembering *God's not willing that any should perish, but that all should come to repentance* - 2 Peter 3:9. Repentance is what He is after, so that your soul should not perish. Experiencing life from that perspective presents a different result. Weigh up your life under His viewpoint. You will see the changes He is asking for you to make today.

A great saying that was in the movie Shawshank Redemption is: "These walls are funny. First you hate them. Then you get used to them. Enough time passes, it gets so you depend on them. That's institutionalised!"

Society is gathering captives who are wide open to tuning into the narrative from media and radical leadership. Our concentration needs to shift into what God conveys, not the governors of the land or the medical sorority. God shaped you, and we belong to Him - that's where our alliance needs to be. *I lift up my eyes to the hills — where does my help come from? My help comes from the LORD, the Maker of heaven and* earth. *Indeed, He who watches over Israel will neither slumber nor sleep* - Psalm 121:1.

The enemy will invariably use love against one another to fight his battle. Looking at the governors of our land, I can perceive they are adopting this same ploy.

"Hunt them down," are the words coming from the Israeli President's mouth! "Hunt down those who are not having the vaccine! It is they who are causing your restrictions of lockdown." WOW.

This was one of Hitler's tactics. And you know how many he slaughtered. There are multitudes who will be persecuted in these last days, it is written.

Brother will betray brother to death, and a father his child; children will rise against their parents and have them put to death. You will be hated by everyone because of My name, but the one who perseveres to the end will be saved. **When they persecute you in one town, flee to the next. Truly I tell you, you will not reach all the towns of Israel before the Son of Man come -.** Matthew 10:21-22.

Threats don't work with God's people. In the end they will claim *I have fought the good fight, I have finished the race; I have kept the faith* - 2 Timothy 4:17.

To the individuals who love and know God, that is their portion. Nothing counts higher to them so *that He might present the church to himself in splendour, without spot or wrinkle or any such thing, that she might be holy and without blemish* - Ephesians 5:27. The church isn't one brand of building that holds individuals on Sunday; it's a people who have overcome. When the Lord comes, He will only observe the heart of man, not the works of man. We, as a Holy people, need to follow our heart. Not the speeches of the world!

It's rare in our everyday existence to witness greatness. Greatness isn't pride or arrogance or the treasures you gain on earth. To those who overcame, just as Jesus Christ overcame, greatness will live in them. Those who have come last, will be first when the last trumpet blasts. *To him who overcomes I will grant to sit with Me on My throne, as I also overcame and sat down with My Father on His throne* - Revelation 3:21.

To the overcomers who have made themselves ready: *These are they that came out of great tribulation, and have washed their robes and made them white in the blood of the Lamb* - Revelation 7:14. Holy people recognise what is significant in this world and the afterlife. Our plight hasn't been to achieve greatness in the earth but to overcome the world and all its trappings. We have our heart set on things above, knowing who is in charge of both.

There are four stages of these final days, as God's people know them. But all stages come under 'The End Times'.

Stage 1: *For the time is come that judgment must begin at the house of God: and if it first begins at us, what shall the end be of them that obey not the gospel of God?* - 1Peter 4:17. This judgement has passed.

Stage 2: *And ye shall hear of wars and rumours of wars: see that ye be not troubled: for all these things must come to pass, but the end is not yet. For nation shall rise against nation, and kingdom against kingdom: and there shall be famines, and pestilences, and earthquakes, in diverse' places. All these are the beginning of sorrows* - Matthew 24:4-8. **This is the stage we are in now in year 2021!**

Stage 3: Tribulation - *that no man might buy or sell, save he that had the mark or the name of the beast or the number of his name* - Revelation 13:7. This scripture is about the QR code that is enforced in all shops. You cannot buy or sell unless you have this mark. *Ugly, festering sores broke out on the people who had the mark of the beast and worshiped its image* - Revelation 16:2. The governors are preparing people to have vaccinations in mass droves. When they have refined this process, they will embed a magnetic tracking device, which will save all your medical documents, economic and social security details.

Stage 4: If, by this point if you haven't turned to God as your Father and repented, you will encounter the wrath of God. The wrath of God is where He will split his people from the rebellious still left on earth. He says when the last trumpet sounds, He will remove His people. He further mentions, *these are they that came out of great tribulation, and have washed their robes and made them white in the blood of the Lamb* - Revelation 7:14.

What does the wrath of God look like?

The anger of God is not something that resides in Him by nature; it is a response to evil. It is provoked! 'God is love'. That is his nature. If there were no sin in the world, there would be no wrath in God. The wrath of God is His judgement on the remaining humans who still haven't turned aside from their sins. These people turn to God and curse Him, they have hardened their hearts even more. The wrath of God will be comparable to what arose in Egypt when God withdrew His people from Pharaoh. The sores will break out on the skin - the rivers turn red, the sun will darken, and the economy will fail. Giant hailstones weighing around 100 pounds will plummet onto the planet. *A third of the living creatures in the sea died, and a third of the ships were destroyed* - Revelation 8:9.

All they have to do is turn to God and repent, but they don't. God's only desire is that no man shall perish that's why He pours out His wrath. No other reason!

To be born in these days is the most privileged time in history. To be witness to a conclusion of an age is extraordinary. ***Unless the Lord had shortened those days, no life would have been saved; but for the sake of the elect, whom He chose, He shortened the days* - Mark 13:20.** Yes, there is an elect group of people living on the earth who have overcome their lives. They were judged in the first judgement, the household of God. Knowing they were prepared for a time such as this. *For many are called, but few are chosen* - Matthew 22:14.

Demonic deception just prior to Jesus' Second Coming will become so great, even the elect would be deceived if it were possible. ***"Who will bring a charge against God's elect? God is the one who justifies* - Romans 8:33.** The elect can rest knowing that their faith in their Lord Jesus Christ has redeemed them from eternal damnation, regardless of what men think or say.

So, as those who have been chosen of God, Holy and beloved, put on a heart of compassion, kindness, humility, gentleness and patience; bearing with one another, and forgiving each other, whoever has a complaint against anyone; just as the Lord forgave you, so also should you. Beyond all these things put on love, which is the perfect bond of unity. Let the peace of Christ rule in your hearts, to which indeed you were called in one body; and be thankful - **Colossians 3:12-15.**

"We live between the act of awakening and the act of surrender. Each morning we awaken to the light and the invitation to a new day and time. At night we surrender to the dark to be taken to play in the world of dreams where time is no more. At birth, we were awakened and emerged to become visible in the world. And at death, we will surrender again to the dark and become invisible." These words were written by my favourite author John O'Donohue. Born in 1956 in Ireland, he was a Philosopher, Poet, Mystic, Author, Priest. Writing this book not only have I experienced every word written, I have researched over fifty authors who claim to carry Holiness. This man John O'Donohue has to be the closest to Holiness that I came across.

Saint John of the Cross another Mystic, Priest, Author and a Carmelite friar born in the 1500s carried what I would call Christ's presence. He had such revelation on the book of Song of Solomon that I listened to it six times. The depth of the revelation engaged me more and more. Such Holiness I have never seen upon one man. Holiness is the highest attainment one person could reach in this lifetime. It's beyond knowledge, possessions, titles, and where we live. I live for this one thing: *I will see Your face in righteousness; I shall be satisfied when I awake in Your likeness* - Psalm 17:15.

To wake up in His likeness and image would be unbelievable. Sometimes I see Him in me and me in Him, which spurts me on for the prize. When I sit with some people, I know my thinking doesn't align with their thinking anymore. Nor do their ways align with the way I live. *See, darkness covers the earth and thick darkness is over the peoples, but the LORD rises upon you and his glory appears over you* - Isaiah 60:2.

I talk about Christ all the time, and no other thing or subject takes my attention. He is why I live and the reason I take my next breath. He is the reason I came to earth and the reason I will leave earth. I don't try to make up the next plan anymore because it is futile when *He makes known the end from the beginning, from ancient times, what is still to come. I say, 'My purpose will stand, and I will do all that I please'* - Isaiah 46:10.

Our thought patterns are the blocking point stopping us from developing into the expression of God on earth. I have recognised a few types of thinking which all create different results in people's lives.

The emotional thinker often has fear and selfishness attached, which leads to hardship and abuse. An irrational thinker brings calamities upon themselves, as does a revenge thinker. An evil thinker is egotistical, insane, hateful, and selfish, which causes violence to others, such as murder and lies.

A compromised thinker has thrown every modern thought into the mix and becomes lukewarm. *Because you are lukewarm–neither hot nor cold–I am about to spit you out of my mouth* - Revelation 3:16.

A logical, rational thinker has examined the start to the end - they have weighed up their judgment and they identify the risks associated. But that doesn't consistently work out the way it's planned because we have evil, selfish, irrational thinkers who may have to be part of the plan. *Be not unequally yoked together with unbelievers: for what fellowship has righteousness with unrighteousness? And what communion has light with darkness?* - 2 Corinthians 6:14.

A righteous thinker or godly person passes all their thoughts up the flagpole of God. *Commit to the LORD whatever you do, and He will establish your plans* - Proverbs 16:3.

This pathway has worked in my life, following the Lord and committing my plans to Him. Most of those plans have come to naught. He sealed the door! But it released me from abuse and sorrow. I would have incurred hardship if I had carried out what I selfishly wished to achieve. It has been part of the overcoming process. Be prepared that your ideas and plans may come to naught.

Plans are merely thoughts until they have been settled. *Your eyes saw me when I was formless; all my days were written in your book and planned before a single one of them began* - Psalm 139:16. Ask for the day that He has written in His book. His plans are higher because He can determine the beginning from the end. The more I look to Him, the freer I become.

In the last days, God writes about seven churches. I think it is essential to know which of these you fit into. Keeping in mind that the church is a metaphor for God's people or His bride, it's not a building.

Church 1: *The church that has abandoned His love and His teachings* - Revelation 2:1-7. In scripture, this church is called Ephesus. It was a prominent commercial and cultural centre. The people were praised for their hard work and perseverance, but they had forsaken their first love, Christ.

Church 2: *The church that remains faithful amidst persecution* - Revelation 2:8-11. Christ does not reprimand this church but warns of impending imprisonment for some of its members, urging them to remain faithful "even to the point of death" and remember the promise of their 'victor's crown'.

Church 3: **The Church that Compromises Its Beliefs - Revelation 2:12.** The city of Pergamum was renowned for its pagan practices. It's easy to normalize the non-Christian behaviour of those around us and allow that behaviour to dilute our values.

Church 4: **The Church that Follows False Prophets - Revelation 2:18-29.** The church's downfall was its devotion to a false prophet that led some members to commit idolatry and immorality. As a result, today many have fallen prey to cult leaders, occult practices, and other false teachings.

Church 5: **The Church that is Spiritually Dead -Revelation 3:1-6.** Our Lord faults the church in Sardis for maintaining an outward appearance of being 'alive,' while being spiritually dead.

Church 6: **The Church that Patiently Endured Despite Weaknesses - Revelation 3:7.** Jesus does not reproach this congregation but condemns its persecutors. Christ promises that if Philadelphia's congregants remain faithful to Him, He will protect them from the 'hour of trial' and make them pillars in God's heavenly temple.

Church 7: *The Church with a Lukewarm Faith* - **Revelation 3:14-22.** Jesus' letter to this church wastes no time denouncing the congregation for its lukewarm faith, threatening to 'spit' the congregation out of His mouth.

Only two churches are worthy in these last days - the persecuted church and the church that patiently endures despite weaknesses. God leaves room in all churches to repent and come away from the sins of those churches. Just remember the word church is a metaphor for groups of people. People are the church, not a building.

Did you notice God will keep the body of people who endure from the 'hour of trial'? The hour of trial is mounting the curve in our world. Rethink your position and change your mind. I have an old saying, "To change your world you change your mind." That's all you have to do!

Your belief system that holds you is like an anchor. You can always lift anchor and move. Every place where your foot treads can change your direction. It's a simple change of the mind! And when your mind adjusts to your new thought, your foot will follow.

Just as there is an inner and outer world within us, God also has a new world wanting to come to earth. *In the beginning God made the heavens and the earth* - Genesis 1:1. This earth He gave to mankind to be stewards and have dominion over all living creatures. We haven't stewarded the earth well, nor have we been good landlords or neighbours to one another. God already grieved over humanity when He sent the flood back in Noah's time. He was like a grieving parent, disappointed in what sins we brought into the world. His decision to allow mankind to live is still playing out in the last days. He had specific promises that need fulfilling before He could end the time frame of this civilization.

Once again, we have brought so much sin into the earth. But this time, God has a different plan! He intends to redeem His saints and gather them in the air. *For the Lord Himself will come down from heaven, with a loud command, with the voice of the archangel and with the trumpet call of God, and the dead in Christ will rise first* - 1Thessalonians 4:16. The graves will be open, and the dead will rise. As I have outlined previously in the seven churches, the persecuted church are these people - they were given 'The Crown of life'. The others who are gathered are the ones who have endured patiently and remained faithful. *We who are still alive and are left will be caught up together with them in the clouds to meet the Lord in the air. And so, we will be with the Lord forever* - 1 Thessalonians 4:17. *These are they that came out of the great tribulation, and have washed their robes and made them white in the blood of the Lamb* - Revelation 7:14.

The washing of your robes means turning away from our sinful nature and overcoming in the name of Our Lord Jesus Christ, having no other gods before their eyes. Loving the Lord God with all their heart, mind, and body, and having their eyes fixed on Him who created all things! *I saw the Holy City, the new Jerusalem, coming down out of heaven from God, prepared as a bride beautifully dressed for her husband* - Revelation 21:2.

These individuals gathered in the clouds or air to meet the Lord will become part of the new Jerusalem coming down out of heaven with the Lord. *Blessed and Holy are those who share in the first resurrection. The second death has no power over them, but they will be priests of God and of Christ and will reign with him for a thousand years* - Revelation 20:6. This thousand-year reign is on the earth as the devil has been locked up in the abyss.

Anybody who remains on the earth after the great tribulation will encounter God's wrath. The saints with Christ will reign together upon the earth. *Look! God's dwelling place is now among the people, and He will dwell with them. They will be His people, and God himself will be with them and be their God. 'He will wipe every tear from their eyes. There will be no more death' or mourning or crying or pain, for the old order of things has passed away* - Revelation 21.

The beauty of God always captures me. At the beginning of time on earth, God had a plan! His time is outside our time, a thousand years is like one day in our time. So, we are in the seven days of His time. When He first spoke creation into existence that took seven days. All His promises will be fulfilled, and yes, God is the winner in the end.

Chapter 5

The Fall and Redemption

God cast Satan out of heaven onto the earth with thousands of angels. Satan's heart shifted into pride on account of his beauty. Satan had the best position in paradise; he was the worship leader. He believed he was God, and pride entered. Many humans have wondered why God dropped him to earth where He was about to present humanity? God needed a people who will reign with Him, so He put them around temptation.

Humanity took the temptation, and now they have seventy, eighty years on earth to overcome their own sinful nature.

The thief comes only to steal and kill and destroy - John 10:10. The devil is the thief, and he's been doing a decent job of plundering, stealing, and destroying since Adam and Eve were first put in the Garden. Satan and his cohorts are giving society a good push in these days, seeing how many people he can corrupt before he gets locked up in the Abyss. He knows his fate in the end.

God has always been in charge! *Wherein in time past ye walked according to the course of this world, according to the prince of the power of the air, the spirit that now works in the children of disobedience* - Ephesians 2:2.

The son of perdition and the followers of Satan will suffer with him in eternity. *But the cowardly, the unbelieving, the vile, the murderers, the sexually immoral, those who practice magic arts, the idolaters and all liars, —they will be consigned to the fiery lake of burning sulphur* - Revelation 21:8. This is called the second death. This death is reserved for unbelievers. Those experiencing this death are all those whose names are not written in the Book of Life. The final judgment, or the lake of fire, is the time when Christ and His Bride returns to the earth. Abel, the original murder victim, is frequently regarded as the original martyr, while Cain, the first murderer, is sometimes identified as a forefather of evil - that's called the first death.

As we know it through scripture, the end time is for the individuals who have fallen from Grace. It's their redemption plan! From Genesis through to Revelation it is the same message, Redeem, Sanctify and Glorify. It's all about saving humankind from the lake of fire. But if you are hell-bent on following sin, there is eternal damnation waiting. This teaching throughout the institutional church has been diluted or not mentioned nowadays. The old church spoke about damnation, and it alarmed many individuals, and they departed from the church houses.

I've noticed society has changed the word sin and renamed it diversity or political correctness. I don't even pick up the term sin being discussed nowadays. If you claim something is diverse, then you aren't announcing it as sin. I wrote a book called 'Political Correctness Is A False God'. I never produced this writing out in society, but it was all about the difference between man's mind and God's mind. Political correctness is the mind of man, the same as the word diversity. God was straightforward and definite about sin.

God allowed Lot and his family to depart from Sodom and Gomorrah before the cities were smitten with fire. There was so much sin in those cities that God could only detect one righteous man. That was Lot! God blesses our families, so the family escaped as long as they didn't turn back into the world they came from.

Noah, the same thing! The flood washed away all the people. Only Noah and his family escaped.

God gave the Israelites forty years before opening the earth in the desert, and the ground swallowed them. Only three got through to the promised land out of two million people.

God has given our society plenty of time to come out of the world. Now it's our time to repent before it's too late. Throughout all history, humanity has had the wrong city in their eyes. The City of the Lord should take our attention away from our present society.

Love not the world, neither the things that are in the world. If any man loves the world, the love of the Father is not in him. For all that is in the world, the lust of the flesh, and the lust of the eyes, and the pride of life, is not of the Father, but is of the world. And the world passes away, and the lust thereof: but he that does the will of God abides forever - 1 John 2:15.

Be alert and of sober mind. Your enemy the devil prowls around like a roaring lion looking for someone to devour - 1 Peter 5:8. Opening our mind to the brainwashing of the world and their logic will cause you to be devoured. *Not thieves nor the greedy nor drunkards nor slanderers nor swindlers will inherit the kingdom of God* - 1 Corinthians 6:10.

Today's culture is encouraged to party, get drunk, sleep around and put down everybody who doesn't think as they do. They're encouraged to take advantage of people in business - lying to one another. If someone speaks contrary, they lower themselves by calling names; this is bullying. In court places, criminals are being set loose and the innocent imprisoned. *Woe to those who call evil good and good evil, who put darkness for light and light for darkness, who put bitter for sweet and sweet for bitter* - Isaiah 5:20.

People are confused and calling good evil and evil good. Neighbour is against neighbour, but understand this. *That in the last days there will come times of difficulty. For people will be lovers of self, lovers of money, proud, arrogant, abusive, disobedient to their parents, ungrateful, unholy, heartless, unappeasable, slanderous, without self-control, brutal, not loving good, treacherous, reckless, swollen with conceit, lovers of pleasure rather than lovers of God, appearing to be godly, but denying its power. Avoid such people* - 2 Timothy 3:1-5.

That which has been hidden will be revealed in these last days. The Glory of God will burst forth over humanity. *Arise, shine, for your light has come, and the glory of the LORD rises upon you* - Isaiah 60:1. As I have touched on before, the Glory is for all, but it will be as a heavyweight if you have sin in your life.

The fear of God is missing in people's lives. *The fear of the Lord is the beginning of wisdom: and the knowledge of the holy one is understanding* - Proverbs 9:11. This surely refers to the foolish virgins with no oil in their lamp on the Lord's return. How many conversations are you invited to have that have no importance to anything? *Let no corrupt word proceed out of your mouth, but what is good for necessary edification, that it may impart grace to the hearers* - Ephesians 4:29.

But I tell you that everyone will give an account on the day of judgment for every empty word they have spoken - Matthew 12:36. Think about that one! How many meaningless conversations do you have? Woe, this made me rethink my words. Today, if someone starts a conversation and isn't near God, I steer the conversation to the Lord's wisdom and understanding. We all stand under this judgement, not just the righteous.

Restoring my trust was a huge overcoming difficulty. The scripture reveals *it's better to trust in the LORD than to put confidence in man. It is better to trust in the LORD than to put confidence in princes* - Psalm 118:8-9. Princes nowadays suggest to me governments.

Our trust was breached in the Garden when Adam and Eve disobeyed God. That breach developed in every individual life upon the planet. That untrustworthy spirit attracts other spirits with the same transgression. And there it is! Another abuse waiting to materialize. God allows us to draw our weakness into our world so we can recognise and overcome them. If you're married or in a relationship, the Lord says *it's as iron sharpens iron, so one person sharpens another* - Proverbs 27:17. Many people just switch from one person to another in relationships. They will invariably encounter the same weaknesses in the next individual if they haven't overcome the defect within themselves.

Once transgression took place in the Garden of God, fear invaded humanity. Fear is the heftiest stopper in mortals. The devil uses this tool of fear-mongering. Take notice of your mind and count the worries you have. I seized every thought captive and overcame my own fears when I went out into the bush for seven years by myself. Imagine the dreads that come upon a woman by herself out in the no where's land of Australia. That was me! I conquered the fear of man in that place and reconstructed my trust in the Lord. Every night and day, I would trust knowing *in peace I will lie down and sleep, for you alone, LORD, make me dwell in safety* - Psalm 4:8. I confessed with my mouth and believed in the Lord that His word is reliable. It turns out it was and is true because every night I laid down, I slept in peace, appreciating the Lord would preserve me. I would wake up every morning knowing that *His angels had charge over you, to keep you in all your ways. In their hands they shall bear you up, lest you dash your foot against a stone* - Psalm 91:11-12. If you don't learn the Lord's Word, you will never become free to live a peaceful, unlimited, quiet life upon the earth. It's imperative to *trust in the Lord with all your heart and lean not on your own understanding; in all your ways submit to Him, and He will make your paths straight* - Proverbs 3:5-6.

I don't always know the way to walk in life. But I do trust in Him who wrote every day in the book of life. Today is all that I have! So that's where I live, not in tomorrow and not in yesterday. Moment by moment! If we don't stay in the minute, we will never enjoy life now. *Whereas you do not know what will happen tomorrow. For what is your life? It is even a vapor that appears for a little time and then vanishes away* - James 4:14.

Pride gets thrown out the window when you look at that scripture. We are but a vapour. A puff of smoke! What confounds me is that the indescribable creator of the universe cherishes that vapour. That vapour has purpose and meaning to God. It gets renamed when it leaves earth and returns to the Father. *To him who overcomes, to him I will give some of the hidden manna, and I will give him a white stone, and a new name written on the stone which no one knows but he who receives it* - Revelation 2:17.

A new name and a new body and reigning and ruling with Him who sent us to the earth - that's a great promise for those who overcome. It's a worthy plight! There's a big universe that God has been planning and waiting for the story of earth to be rolled up. *Then the sky receded as a scroll when it is rolled up, and every mountain and island was moved out of its place* - Revelation 6:14.

Every story has a beginning and an end, so does the earth. We are the seed carriers! *I planted the seed, another watered it, but God has been making it grow* - 1 Corinthian 3:6. There is no pride in that statement! We are His special possession here on earth, a Holy people. Eternity is a very long time to be alive in this life and the other lives still to come. Remember we came from Him. *Before I formed you in the womb I knew you, before you were born I set you apart; I appointed you as a prophet to the nations* - Jeremiah 1:5.

A prophet is someone who goes before and makes a way so others can follow. Jesus Christ was a prophet. He was also God incarnated upon the earth through His Son, and that makes Him the Messiah. He made way for all mankind to be redeemed by laying His life down as a sacrifice. God asks us to do the same, lay our life down so He can have full reign of the life upon the earth. *Therefore, I urge you, brothers and sisters, in view of God's mercy, to offer your bodies as a living sacrifice, Holy and pleasing to God—this is your true and proper worship* - Romans 12:1.

If it's good enough for Jesus Christ it's good enough for us to give over the life to who created the life. Who wrote the life! And placed its days in 'The Book of Life'. I would think He knows more than me. It's pride that says He doesn't!

Jesus Christ went against the synagogue and the leaders because He knew more than they did. This threatened them so they had Him crucified. Little did they know that the crucifixion was ordained by God the Father. Jesus was the sacrificial lamb who was slain. He was God's way to redeem mankind.

I believe all of us have had the opportunity in this life to hear and see God the Father and Jesus Christ's perfect plan for humanity. People divert away from this door of redemption because they know they have to overcome their sinful nature. The track of overcoming seems too hard, so they go back into their own life with the knowledge that God exists, but they leave Him there. Others say they don't believe, but I can see that's a lie. They don't want to follow His ways. They would prefer to take that 'free will' and call life theirs. That's pride!

At the beginning of my walk with Christ I understood that 'free will" isn't free until its inside of God's will. Outside His will is rebellion! That's taking it back to Adam and Eve once again - they had 'free will' but traded it for rebellion. To come back into that perfect place within the Garden of God, we need to take up the cross of Jesus Christ and follow Him. *Enter through the narrow gate. For wide is the gate and broad is the road that leads to destruction, and many enter through it* - Matthew 7:13. *Only a few find it* - Mathew 7:14. Wow only a few find this gate! I wanted to be the few. I wanted to be worthy to stand before the creator of the universe and give an account of my life. *Not everyone who says to Me, 'Lord, Lord,' shall enter the kingdom of heaven, but he who does the will of My Father in heaven. Many will say to Me in that day, 'Lord, Lord, have we not prophesied in Your name, cast out demons in Your name, and done many wonders in Your name?' And then I will declare to them, 'I never knew you; depart from Me, you who practice lawlessness'* - Matthew 7:21-23.

That one scripture has enough depth to transform any sinner to follow Christ. Yet they don't; they harden their hearts. Anything in life that is worthy of having isn't easy. It takes guts, faith, perseverance, endurance, and sacrifice - it's the narrow way. Sometimes it felt like I was walking on the edge of a cliff with a blindfold on. God always made sure I got through. How would it be if He let us fall! *For He will command his angels concerning you to guard you in all your ways* - Psalm 91:11.

Merciful, redeeming, loving, Holy God! If by now you can't see in these writings that He is all that we were looking for in life, then you will look for all those things in other ways but always *fall short of the Glory of God* - Romans 3:23.

Born To Be Holy

Chapter 6

The Glory of God

For many are called, but few are chosen - Matthew 22:14. What an honour to be adopted by the King. To write about His Holiness, to lay down my possessions, to follow Him. I can announce that is an honour! Would you do that for a higher call? Or would you remain with your comfortable lot in life? The rich man came to Jesus and asked what must I do to enter the Kingdom of God? *Jesus told him, Go, sell what you have and give to the poor, and you will have treasure in heaven; and come, follow Me. When the young man heard this, he went away in sorrow, because he had great wealth* - Matthew 19: 21-22. Are you the rich man? Have you got your treasures stashed on earth? *Do not store up for yourselves treasures on earth, where moth and rust destroy, and where thieves break in and steal* - Matthew 6:19. In these last days, it is vital to re-evaluate your world and the eternal life that you will stand in before long.

I am the LORD: that is my name: and My Glory will I not give to another, neither my praise to graven images - Isaiah 42:8. Who is the Lord talking about in that scripture? He is talking about Himself! If He were to give us the Glory, then there would be a miss direction of trust. This is where the institutional churches have failed in the past. The preacher became a rock star, and people looked to them as some sort of leader who should be admired. Whereas they should have been redirecting that praise and Glory to the one who is the Glory. Many have fallen because of this pride. I can see in this 'time of sorrow' as it's known, God's closing the doors of the institutional churches and redeeming the people within those buildings.

Have you noticed in my writings that I call the building the institutional church? That's because I feel they have stolen the name 'church', which is reserved for His Bride. *Not everyone who says to me, 'Lord, Lord,' will enter the kingdom of heaven, but only the one who does the will of my Father who is in heaven* - Matthew 7:21. You can be busy doing Christianity, but are you about the Father's business?

I have met many people outside the institutional church building. When I ask them why they are out the answer comes back, "The walls are too small!" It means they're limited in their teachings and thinking. This is true, but the leaders inside the building don't know it. God, in His redemptive plan, will close the churches and get them out from behind their own safety, and fundamental thinking. When you think you are the answer to the world's problem. That's pride!

On an upside, the institutional church offered me a base in the Word of God. But those walls were restrictive to the overcoming process and being about the Father's business. Jesus Christ lives in humility! Many leaders within the walls of teaching are not humble. They pride themselves on being the leader, and they assume they know more than everybody else. They further think that they need to preserve the humans outside the walls. That's pride! *No one can come to me unless the Father who sent me draws him. And I will raise him up on the last day* - John 6:44. That claims it's the spirit who draws all people to Himself.

I've heard many people say that everybody who isn't in a church building isn't doing the right thing. That's not true! Many people have been called to serve outside the walls. They Love God with their whole heart, mind and strength. They have been hidden by God; they are *a chosen people, a royal priesthood, a holy nation, God's special possession, that you may declare the praises of him who called you out of darkness into his wonderful light* - 1Peter 2:9.

I always weigh myself up against the seven churches in the last days. By doing this it reveals who we are in the big scheme of things. *So then, each of us will give an account of ourselves to God* – Romans 14:12.

Therefore, my beloved, as you have always obeyed, so now, not only as in my presence but much more in my absence, work out your own salvation with fear and trembling, for it is God who works in you, both to will and to work for his good pleasure - Philippians 2:12. It's up to us to work out our own salvation! Laziness and familiarity would give the job to another. Many have done this by turning up on Sunday into the building and experiencing the same comfortable routine.

Seek after His Glory! *For in this tent we groan, longing to put on our heavenly dwelling, if indeed by putting it on we may not be found naked. For while we are still in this tent, we groan, being burdened—not that we would be unclothed, but that we would be further clothed, so that what is mortal may be swallowed up by life* - 2 Corinthians 5:2-4.

His life is swallowing up our life. Our mortal existence is swallowed up by immortality! He who has prepared us gives us a spirit of guarantee. While we are awake in this frame, it limits us to the Glory we can encounter. These mortal bodies cannot bear the perfect measure of His brilliance. Jesus Christ rose in His glorified body from the grave. Moses asked to see God's Glory. God told him that no one can look at His face and live. *For our God is a consuming fire* - Hebrews 12:29. The Glory is too powerful! We're provided a measure of Glory through the Holy Spirit who the Lord sent to us as a helper and comforter.

In this gathering in the air at the last trumpet, with those raised earlier from the grave, we will be given a glorified body from the Lord. This different body will carry the full Glory back to earth when the New City Jerusalem comes out of heaven.

Overcoming our sinful nature offers another measure of glory that passes through our soul and body. *But we all, with unveiled face, beholding as in a mirror the glory of the Lord, are being transformed into the same image from glory to glory, just as from the Lord, the Spirit* - 2 Corinthians 3:18. There is a stage coming that those who have run the race and overcome their life the righteousness will be revealed upon them.

In the last days, God says, I will pour out my Spirit on all people. Your sons and daughters will prophesy, your young men will see visions, your old men will dream dreams - Acts 2:17.

With the adversity of the world, many are falling away from the faith. But then, many are growing into spiritual awakening. Still, I look at many divisions in the body of Christ. People in the institutional church think they are the body of Christ, and nobody outside is eligible to be part of the body. This isn't a truth - it's a deception! Many carry the spirit of God who are not part of the fundamental religious circuit. They don't follow the Christian church; they follow the God of the Christian church. There is a difference, a big difference! I have heard leaders state if we are not part of the congregation, we are breaking the scripture. *Not to abandon our own meeting together, as is the habit of some people, but encouraging one another; and all the more as you see the day drawing near* - Hebrews 10:25.

In my walk with God, He lifted me out of all meetings so I could overcome. I still had individuals to whom I spoke, and our only conversation was God. *For where two or three gathers in my name, there am I with them* - Matthew 18:21. This, to me, declared I didn't forsake the gathering. I was gathered over the phone with like-minded friends. Not everything is a standard formula that all have to follow. The Lord directs our path, not a pastor or teacher who has wanted to keep people in their buildings.

Allowing your mind to think about the affairs of this world, you will miss what God's achieving in the Kingdom on the earth. The two worlds are just like the realms we have within our soul. The outer world and the inner realm! Just as our outer world is passing away, so is this world. *The world and its desires pass away, but whoever does the will of God lives forever* - 1 John 2:17.

Remember, we are just a vapour! Considering or talking about the current conditions on earth will not get you anywhere. It's better to think about things in heaven. That's where your treasure should be at this point.

It's the overcoming process that brings the kingdom to earth - we are carriers of the kingdom. The treasure of God also lives within us so that *every good and perfect gift from above, coming down from the Father of the heavenly lights, who does not change like shifting shadows* - James 1:17. We are the representative of heaven, ambassadors of the King! *Therefore, if anyone is in Christ, he is a new creation. The old has passed away; behold, the new has come* - 2 Corinthians 5:17. There you are, standing on the earth as a new creation, ready to be who you were created to be. You haven't got your old life or the desires in your eyes anymore - you only have eyes for the King and His plans and purposes. I would be happy writing books for the rest of my life sitting next to a river. We are a body of Christ coming to Him in all different ages and abilities. *His divine power has given us everything we need for a godly life through our knowledge of Him who called us by His own glory and goodness* - 2 Peter 1:3.

We have been reconciled through the overcoming of our old life. *All this is from God, who reconciled us to Himself through Christ and gave us the ministry of reconciliation* - 2 Corinthians 5:18.

What is the ministry of reconciliation? The ministry of reconciliation refers to the work believers were given to do and the message they declare. All of us have different roles to carry out upon the earth, but we are one body. 'The body of Christ'. Ambassadors! We are ambassadors not for the earthy kingdom or government but for God's Heavenly Kingdom on earth. So, this reconciliation ministry is all about reconciling people to Jesus Christ and how He ordained you to serve Him on earth. We are carrying the Kingdom of God everywhere we go; it's His embassy. His Holy Spirit! We have all of heaven backing us up. All the protection, all the treasures of heaven, are at your disposal. No plague, no sickness, no disease can enter because it's His kingdom. To have this authority, you needed first to take your own land back, which is your body and life. Then you needed to place it into the hands of the one who made the life and wrote every day in a book.

Your kingdom come, your will be done, on earth as it is in heaven - Matthew 6:10. This is what we were born for, the coming of the King and His kingdom. The healing of every human on earth is the will of God. When Jesus walked the earth, He healed the multitudes. It's His will! *No evil shall be allowed to befall you, no plague will come near your tent* - Psalm 91:10. The world, with its calamities of plagues, needs to understand there is another way, and that way has no sickness nor disease.

The prayers that Jesus prayed: *Our Father which art in heaven, hallowed be thy name. Thy kingdom come, thy will be done in earth, as it is in heaven. Give us this day our daily bread. And forgive us our debts, as we forgive our debtors. And lead us not into temptation, but deliver us from evil: For thine is the kingdom, and the power, and the glory, forever. Amen.* - Matthew 6:9-13.

You can't get any better than those holy words from our Lord! We, as ambassadors, are only to do what we see the Father do. We can't go make up the next plan without knowing His plan!

These last days are certainly causing people to fight! Fight with their neighbours, fight the good fight, and I'm even meeting freedom fighters. None of these things will make a difference in the end. Every battle has a reason! If you concentrate on the fight, you will be hoodwinked from seeing what it was created for. These last days upon earth are to show you WHY! It's your repentance time, nothing more. These fights were created for an opportunity to repent. Everything that happens on earth at this end time period is to turn people around. Get them to look upon Christ, not into the fight.

We're used to doing something! We forget maybe we need to do nothing. The feeling of not doing anything can feel opposed to how we were made. I remember going through nothingness, but what I did was embrace the nothingness, which brought me to see something different from what I had. Something is always on the other side of nothingness! But we don't like the feeling of releasing and letting go. Releasing has a sense of powerlessness. This is why we are powerless. Pride and fear would have us to hold on tight to what we own and what we know. Let Go! Feel the freedom of trusting in Him. This freedom feels like going down a country road in a sports car with the wind in your hair. The sun shines through the trees and sparkles as you drive. That's how I roll, FREEDOM!

We haven't got time left on our side; we are in the last days. *But as the days of Noah were, so shall also the coming of the Son of man be. For as in the days that were before the flood they were eating and drinking, marrying and giving in marriage, until the day that Noah entered into the ark, and knew not until the flood came, and took them all away; so, shall also the coming of the Son of man be* - Matthew 24:37-39. Look out of yourself and your life and look into the Son of God. The time is short!

I've always acknowledged that humans have been trained in all different ways. But there is only one way! *Jesus answered, "I am the way and the truth and the life. No one comes to the Father except through me* - John 14:16.

I have seen God tweak people's understanding to bring them out of their training into Him. It's not the training that will get you to the Father, it's the relationship you have with Our Lord Jesus Christ. *Not everyone who says to me, 'Lord, Lord,' will enter the kingdom of heaven, but only the one who does the will of my Father who is in heaven* - Matthew 7:21. I know I have quoted that scripture before in this book, but to me it is very important that we get this.

New Age thinking has scripture built into their ideologies, so does Buddhism, Judaism, Hinduism, and another fourteen others, including Christianity. We watered most of these teachings down due to man's mind or pride coming in and compromising the Word of God.

Nature speaks or cries out, and the *heavens declare the Glory of God; the skies proclaim the work of his hands* - Psalm 19:1. *The mountains and the hills shall break forth before you into singing, and all the trees of the field shall clap their hands* - Isaiah 55:12. I sit in nature often! Nature always talks and announces, and the land has history written on the earth and atmosphere. The skies declare His glory day and night. Nothing is more intriguing than sitting listening to the day. The Lord is in all creation, but He lives in and behind His creation.

We have a still, soft, small voice that lives in us. Often that voice gets crowded out by the clamour of the world and the noise of your mind. That's why we need to overcome all those noises that flood out the Lord's voice. Remember, He lives in us because we are His creation, just like nature. That still soft voice is the voice of God. We generally reason that voice out due to our learnings. It's important to understand the Word of God so you know who is talking. The world or God! After many years of listening *My sheep hear my voice, and I know them, and they follow me: And I give unto them eternal life; and they shall never perish, neither shall any man pluck them out of my hand* - John 10:27. Never in all my years of sleeping on the rivers of Australia did I feel fearful. I knew the Lord loved me and would protect me. But if you don't know Him you would get fearful. There's a big difference!

Eternal life is about not only knowing the Lord but following Him. *The world and its desires pass away, but whoever does the will of God lives forever* - 1 John 2:17. Eternal life is the never-ending story and the happy ever after story all rolled into one. Most people have a ten-year plan for their life on earth - I have an eternal plan given to me by the Father in heaven. I know my next thousand years have been written after I finish this course upon the earth, called the Tribulation. *Then I saw thrones, and those seated on them were given authority to judge. I also saw the souls of those who had been beheaded for their testimony to Jesus, and for the word of God. They had not worshipped the beast or its image and had not received its mark on their foreheads or their hands. They came to life and reigned with Christ for a thousand years* - Revelation 20:4.

He is an eternal God who makes us an eternal people. We are His creation, and He is in us. *And the two shall become one flesh. So, they are no longer two but one flesh* - Mark 10:8. Overcoming the mind and flesh brings us into the Spirit, and His Spirit is one. We are the bride of Christ, the overcome church, His special possession. That's the ultimate in life! To reach the place of knowing who we were born to be **'Holy just as I am Holy'.** And that's where we started in this book - the journey to be holy.

You can't be something unless you believe you are that something. A King isn't a King unless he believes he is a king. A bride isn't a bride unless she accepts that she is a bride. I believe I am the bride of Christ, and I have reached the rest of Christ within me. *For we which have believed do enter into rest, as he said* - Hebrews 4:3. The next part of that scripture says not all will enter the rest. *So, I swore in My wrath, 'They shall not enter My rest,' although the works were finished from the foundation of the world* - Hebrew 4:3.

God created the world, then *God said, "Let us make man in our image"* - Genesis 1:26. Taking dominion over the creation of your life that reflects His life is the biggest task you will be given whilst living on earth. The path to Holiness was a letting go of self so He could rebuild us into His image. It was letting go of darkness, so the *light shone out of darkness, made His light shine in our hearts to give us the light of the knowledge of God's Glory displayed in the face of Christ* - 2 Corinthians 4:6. It is the knowledge that allows the face of Christ to shine forth, revealing God's glory. If we don't know how the one we are following thinks, how can we be part of this end time harvest. When the Glory is illuminated within it shines, and Christ can be seen. *Arise, shine, for your light has come, and the glory of the LORD rises upon you* - Isaiah 60:1. I have also mentioned this scripture before!

But it all comes back to the same thing walking on earth as a reflection of His Glory. That's why religion will never shine this glory because it's not who He is. We are the church, and we are His Glory! So, religion in God's eyes is looking after the widows and orphans.

At this end-time period people will look for a genuine display of Christ on earth. They all have seen the groups and training arenas, but this will not suffice in this last move of God. The body of Christ is man fully alive on earth, displaying His Glory, and the revelation of Christ is the hope of His glory! Wisdom, understanding, and revelation in God are the keys to success in this life and the afterlife. I was asked once in an interview what is the key to success - my answer was respect. Respect for the plan, respect for those around you and respect for the position you have been given and respect for the organisation. If we don't respect the one who owns all, then who do we respect? *For every animal of the forest is mine, and the cattle on a thousand hills. I know every bird in the mountains, and the creatures of the field are mine. If I were hungry I would not tell you, for the world is mine, and all that is in it* - Psalm 50.

My people are destroyed from lack of knowledge. Because you have rejected knowledge, I also reject you as my priests; because you have ignored the law of your God, I also will ignore your children - Hosea 4:6. We bring everything upon ourselves because we lack knowledge. Order brings the Glory of God. Order in yourself, order in the tasks you have been given. I have seen when order is restored - blessings get poured out. Right now, this world is in chaos; there is anarchy. The compromises people have made in society are bringing tribulation upon themselves. They have done this to themselves - they can't blame God because God is a God of order, not disorder.

The exultation of humanity is the relationship with Christ beyond salvation. What is Zion? It's a temple, a dwelling place, a fortress, the mountain of the Lord, the place where the Lord is enthroned. *In Zion a stone that causes people to stumble and a rock that makes them fall, and the one who believes in him will never be put to shame* - Roman 9:33. Jesus Christ is that cornerstone and we are broken upon His rock. We are His dwelling place, so we are Zion! Our bodies are the temple of Christ. Zion is a spiritual being! *Do you not know that your body is a temple of the Holy Spirit within you, whom you have from God? You are not your own, for you were bought at a price. So, glorify God in your body* - 1 Corinthians 6:19.

Rejoice greatly, Daughter Zion! Shout, Daughter Jerusalem! See, your king comes to you, righteous and victorious, lowly and riding on a donkey, on a colt, the foal of a donkey - Zachariah 9:9. There is a body of Christ and it is called Zion! We limit ourselves by not thinking the way God thinks.

Throughout life, we have chosen what we want instead of what God wants, and this has caused us hardships because it put disorder in our lives. *The Lord is my shepherd; I shall not want* - Psalm 23:1. If you 'want', you haven't come far enough! There is no want in God! If you're living in the rest of God, you have all that you need in the moment. Every moment will take care of itself. *So, do not worry, saying, 'What shall we eat?' or 'What shall we drink?' or 'What shall we wear?'* - Matthew 6:31. Our Heavenly Father knows what we need when we need it. It's all taken care of!

The history of humanity has seen disobedience and rebellion at its fullness. The bottom line of many is bringing disorder into the world. When you have multitudes of people with the same bottom line, then you have anarchy. Anarchy brings judgement upon every one of us! *For in the same way you judge others, you will be judged, and with the measure you use, it will be measured to you* - Matthew 7:2.

When I saw society in recent years breakdown, especially the family unit, I knew this was the nail in the coffin for humanity. I researched throughout all human history and saw the same alarming thing. Sodom and Gomorrah burning down because the sin was so extreme. Sexual sin has become so abnormal that confusion has entered people. The confusion starts as a thought that can sway you to the dark side of the road. You will think it is normal because you have made it normal in your mind.

Let's get back to the beginning! *He created them male and female and blessed them. And He named them 'Mankind' when they were created* - Genesis 5:22. It doesn't mean that these confused people can't be saved, because they can. But it takes a turning away from this sin. Any sin is forgivable if we turn away. *Cursing and lying, murder and stealing, and adultery are rampant; one act of bloodshed follows another.* **Therefore, the land mourns, and all who dwell in it will waste away with the beasts of the field and the birds of the air; even the fish of the sea disappear....** - Hosea 4:2:3. Yes, it's the people who are sinning who are causing these curses to come on the land and its people. The sins of this generation are an abomination in the Lord's eyes. And in mine also! We get used to or don't look at the abominations that are happening around us. But the Lord sees all! Why have we got calamities in the world? It's because of the sins of the people! That's where it's coming from; it is simple, the sins of the people.

It's not a virus that's a plague, not a vaccine that's just a vessel to achieve the outcome required by 'One World government', even though the Chinese must be laughing all the way to the bank. In my view, the virus was manufactured in their laboratories and the anti-vaccine that has a synthetic particle was also manufactured in their labs. Silent but deadly war if you ask me!

Separating the goats and the sheep is a part of the great divide in humanity. *All the nations will be gathered before him, and he will separate the people one from another as a shepherd separates the sheep from the goats* - Matthew 25:32. The tribulation is giving you an opportunity to repent. But saying that, you are deciding for this coming day, today.

God's righteous people or the sheep will be put on the right, and He will put the goats on His left. What have we in the Government right or left? This separation is here now, but it won't be complete until the tribulation is complete. Also, the vaccination that they are forcing upon people is causing a great divide. When we voted for the gay movement to be married, we also separated. Checking out one ingredient in this vaccination, I observed a word called 'Chimera'. The term is derived from Greek mythology, meaning a fire-breathing monster that was part lion, goat, and part dragon. They describe Satan as a fire-breathing dragon and the goats are people who didn't repent of their sins.

Then the King will say to those on his right, Come, you who are blessed by my Father; take your inheritance, the kingdom prepared for you since the creation of the world - Matthew 25:34.

Then He will say to those on his left, depart from me, you who are cursed, into the eternal fire prepared for the devil and his angels - Matthew 25:41.

Choose this day who you will serve?

I'm seeing a significant shift in people through this time of sorrow that is upon humanity. People are considering their first love, Jesus Christ. In my walk with God, I have been shut up, pushed away, and walked out on because people didn't want to hear the Word of God. Nowadays, they want to understand why the world is in such trouble. So, they ask the ones who carry His Word in their heart. God's Word aligns with the happenings in the world. It says just one factor, REPENT the time is near for his return of His bride who will come out of the great tribulation. This time of sorrow and tribulation is the end of time as we know it on the earth. We have to move away from seeing life with our carnal understanding and come back into the spirit of God. Seeing from the viewpoint of God, you will perceive the signs of the times are here.

We have four speaking mountains at the moment: media, government, medical, and military/police. They deliver the same terminology: fear and control. These crafted identities have one thought in common. To terrify and throw down everything that challenges their agenda. These mountains, identified by biblical writings, are assigned to larger identities with one factor in mind. To outwork the 'One World Government'. This strategy has been in action since 1920s, but quickened in these present days. Their plan is to dominate the economy and the people. We are identifiable with our phones, and these new QR scans put us under the watchful eye of governing bodies. The vaccination they are trying to enforce has magnetic properties that are receivable through the 5G towers placed around the cities. The modern cars have computer chips that can be immobilized by these towers. A magnetic pulse coming from these towers connects to the magnetic material in these vaccines and can immobilise any person. It is said to slow people down in their minds to become compliant. Its long-term effects can control humans. Control the race, and you can depopulate the ones the government feels are unworthy to be on the planet.

The 5G network works by using higher frequencies on the electromagnetic spectrum. The frequencies range from 3.5

gigahertz (GHz). Before 5G was launched, these higher frequencies weren't used in mobile networks. Instead, they are typically used in devices like security scanners.

We are under the surveillance of the 'One World Order' being rolled out into society. It's time to get your brain out of the world and into God's world. Our hearts and minds need to think outside these mountains into God's mountain.

Come out of her, my people, be not partakers of her sins, and receive not of her plagues - Revelation 18:4.

The plague of Covid is just the beginning!

God's plan will meet the World Government's plan. The government's judgement upon humanity will backfire. The tribulation time will see the evil, corrupt plan ending after seven years. My calculation, puts the end at 2026.

Here is wisdom: The one who has understanding must calculate the number of the beast, because it is the number of a man. His number is 666. *Whoever has ears, let them hear what the Spirit says to the churches* - Revelation 13:18. The barcodes that we scan every day have this number 666 implanted in them.

Another area, which I felt we need to examine, is mediums or fortune-tellers.

There shall not be found among you anyone who burns his son or his daughter as an offering. Anyone who practices divination or tells fortunes or interprets omens, or a sorcerer or a charmer or a medium. Or a necromancer or one who inquires of the dead, for whoever does these things is an abomination to the Lord. And because of these abominations the Lord your God is driving them out before you - Deuteronomy 18:10-12.

Abortions have reached a new peak when you can kill a baby at birth. This is offering your sons and daughters as offerings on the altar of darkness.

People flock to fortune-tellers hoping to have a glimpse of their future. This also is a deception! Demons can talk and give the answers to what you want to hear.

Necromancy is the practice of magic involving communication with the dead either by summoning their spirits as apparitions, visions or raising them bodily for the purpose of divination, imparting the means to foretell future events, discover hidden knowledge, to bring someone back from the dead.

All these things are as an abomination!

Beware of false prophets, who come to you in sheep's clothing but inwardly are ravenous wolves - Matthew 7:15.

And I will bless them that bless you, and curse him that curse you: and in you shall all families of the earth be blessed - Genesis 12:3. Words of condemnation and judgement will be turned back on our accusers. It's a promise of the Lord!

We need to recognise when these false prophets have hoodwinked us by knowing the Word of God! Once they have been recognised, a prayer to the Father in Heaven will reverse any curse, hexes, or spells they have sent your way.

The clouds are rolling in on this present world! Satan will give it a proper shove with His fallen black angels to apprehend and capture as many souls as he can before he is locked up in the pit or abyss for a thousand years.

The fog on our windshield will clear as we grasp the end-time revelations that are written for us to arm ourselves as we pass through the tribulation. Revelation means it needs to be uncovered, as it is behind a veil.

I want to arm you with what is coming!

The virus is a distraction from what the governing bodies are doing. But in saying that, it is a plague! And that is part of this end-time happening. The economy was the focus, and this vaccination becomes the vehicle to stop us from buying or selling. *And that no man might buy or sell, that had the mark, or the name of the beast, or the number of his name* - Revelation 13:17.

You will hear of wars and rumours of wars, but see to it that you are not alarmed. These things must happen, but the end is still to come. Nation will rise against nation, and kingdom against kingdom. There will be famines and earthquakes in various places. All these are the beginning of birth pains- Matthew 24:7.

It's only the beginning!

An ugly and painful sore broke out on the people who had the mark of the beast and worshiped his image - Revelation 16:1. I am hearing people are breaking out in shingles through this vaccination. Shingles isn't just a nasty and painful experience. It can also cause strokes and heart attacks.

There are seven trumpets that sound from heaven in these last days. These trumpets have seven angels with bowls, and each bowl carries extreme anguish for humanity. Why is God doing this? Because it's the end of time as we know it! God values this time to turn people back to Him. Remember, His only desire is that no man shall perish. People need a good wake up call.

After this temporary interlude called the 'Time of Sorrows' we will endure the tribulation. I will share that time with its experiences.

The seven angels with the seven bowls!

First Angel: *The first angel sounded his trumpet, and there came hail and fire mixed with blood, and it was hurled down on the earth. A third of the earth was burned up, a third of the trees were burned up, and all the green grass was burned up"* - Revelations 8:7.

Second Angel: *The second angel sounded his trumpet, and something like a huge mountain, all ablaze, was thrown into the sea. A third of the sea turned into blood, a third of the living creatures in the sea died, and a third of the ships were destroyed"* - Revelation 8:8-9.

Third Angel: *The third angel sounded his trumpet, and a great star, blazing like a torch, fell from the sky on a third of the rivers and on the springs of water. The name of the star is Wormwood. A third of the waters turned bitter, and many people died from the waters that had become bitter* - Revelation 8:10.

Fourth Angel: *The fourth angel sounded his trumpet, and a third of the sun was struck, a third of the moon, and a third of the stars, so that a third of them turned dark. A third of the day was without light, and also a third of the night* - Revelation 8:12.

God is bringing these judgments to those who haven't repented. So, all those people out there that are doing their own thing, you have brought this upon humanity. After blowing the fourth trumpet, there is a brief pause before the last three trumpets are blown.

The fourth voice came from heaven saying, *'Woe! Woe! Woe to the inhabitants of the earth, because of the trumpet blasts about to be sounded by the other three angels!'*

Fifth Angel: *The fifth trumpet (and the first woe) results in a terrifying plague of "demonic locusts" that attack and torture for five months.* The plague begins with a star falling from heaven. The angel is given 'the key to the shaft of the Abyss'. By this time an angel has come and marked God's people so this plague shall not touch them. He opens the Abyss, releasing a horde of 'locusts' with 'power like that of scorpions. The locusts do not touch the plant life of earth; instead, they head straight for 'those people who did not have the seal of God on their foreheads'. For five months, these locusts torment people, whose agony is so great that they will wish to die, 'but death will elude them'. The locusts may not kill anyone, only torture them.

As Clint eastward would say, "Are you feeling lucky?"

Sixth Angel: *The sixth trumpet (and the second woe) involves the onslaught of another demonic horde.* A voice from the altar of God calls for the release of the four angels who are bound - **these are fallen angels. These four angels had been kept in captivity for just this purpose: to wreak destruction during the tribulation. Remember, God** owns the keys to heaven and hell, so He has keys at His disposal. The wicked angels lead a supernatural cavalry of thousands upon thousands to kill a third of humanity.

Despite the severity and horror of these plagues, the survivors on earth still refuse to repent. Instead, they continue in their idolatry, murder, sorcery, sexual immorality, and their theft.

Seventh Angel: *The seventh trumpet (and the third woe) sounds, and immediately there are loud voices in heaven saying, "The kingdom of the world has become the kingdom of our Lord and of his Messiah, and he will reign for ever and ever."*

God will lock the devil up so he can't harm the people anymore. So, all turns out well for those who love our Lord Jesus Christ as their saviour. This society is passing away as is the evil devil and his fallen angels.

Repent this day, for the Kingdom of God is near!

Final word

We all have our walk upon the earth, and they all differ from the next person. Some come under the heading of evil, others under religion, and still others walk with no constraints of belonging to any crowd. Not one person is better than another. They just haven't seen life from where you stand. In my case, I saw life from the religious and evil, so I decided to walk where nobody was so I could be who I was called to be. Still that does not make me better than another.

We all have different ways of speaking, and we all have different ways of perceiving. Still, no person is better than the next. People talk to others from the level on which they stand, I speak from where I stand. All are important; no one is better than the other. We are all made in God's image, but not all have reached that image. Still nobody is better than another.

When I look back over my walk with God, it is the most unusual walk I have seen a person live. To live nowhere but everywhere it's unique, even for me to say. Someone knocked at the door today at where I have been staying for the last five weeks writing this book. She said you must be sad that it's nearly time to move on. I replied with honesty, "Oh no I will finish what I came to do." I have been warm, and comfortable and I am grateful. With no particular plan, just a thought, I will go to the next part of life with no concern. I know after twelve years of living like this, the next piece of life turns up. And it's not always what I thought it would be. So, I leave it up to God to make a way and show me the way. The plan is in His hand.

If you're reading this last message that means you have read some or all of my writings. I have enjoyed writing about the process that it took to overcome my life and portray those experiences to you. I think the crucial part of life is the understanding of life. That's been my plight to understand what is the purpose of mankind. Also, to understand the creator of the universe and how He thinks! His thoughts are higher than our thoughts.

The few friends I have found along the way have been such a delight. I had to learn how to be a friend to them so I could learn how to be a friend to myself. They were better at being a friend than I was. But they loved me and were willing to allow me to learn from my weakness.

I had a lady hurl abuse at me the other day because I wrote something that touched her weaknesses. If we can touch others in their weaknesses, that's alright because that's what Jesus did. Jesus sat with the sinners but told them how it was; giving them a chance to turn from their wicked ways. He wasn't out to win friends; He was out to show them the way back home to the Father. People who know me say that I'm a straight shooter - I say it without concern for political correctness. I know whose world I can speak into and whose I cannot.

I've been kicked out of most churches in my life because I disagreed with a part of a doctrine that was getting preached on the day. I was never one to keep my mouth shut. Nowadays I'm tamer; time heals all things. In the end I just stopped going to church because my walk took me to the great outback of Australia. I have poked my head into one or two churches along the way, but it's not for me anymore. Once the walls and the roof were taken off the church, I found it was much freer just being with God everywhere and nowhere.

I have never taken my face away from His face, and I look into His Word when needing wisdom that isn't already written on my heart. Most of His Word is in my heart nowadays, and I know how He thinks about most things. As you might have noticed, I'm not shy about saying what is written in His Word. He gave me a voice! If people don't like what I say, that's okay. It is written and maybe it's time for that piece of God to be heard!

I want to write about 'the Bride of Christ if God gives me that opportunity. If He doesn't, then so be it! I have noticed that my writing has come after I have experienced the pain of each word written. My first book, 'How I overcame my own life' was written on my phone as I travelled for the first three and half years of my journey travelling Australia. I would send each piece of writing to myself, and when I was in range of the Internet, I would piece them together. It's been six years since I wrote that book because I had to walk the overcoming process out, so I became whom I was writing about. If the Lord commissions me to write about the Bride of Christ, then that will be my next walk.

I believe with all my heart that is the call for humanity upon the earth. He speaks of His Bride from Genesis through to Revelation. The bride is the true church, not the organised church. Some who are in the organised church will be part of this bridal party, but not all. The invitation goes beyond their walls to the greater body of Christ. When the Lord comes back, He will take one from there and one from there. He is after the heart of man, not the works of man! Many will say, "Lord, Lord, didn't I cast out demons in your name?" And He will say, "Get away from me because I didn't know you."

The Lord is after the relationship, not the works. That's the Bride who has made herself ready for His return.

It's important to weigh yourself against the seven churches in the last days. I have written about them in this book. You will see where you stand and what the Lord may have against you.

Time is short upon the earth. We are in the End Times and the time of sorrow and tribulation. We're in 2021, I would say we have five and three-quarters years of time up our sleeve before the return of Christ, but no man knows the day or the hour. As I have written, it's going to get very rocky in the coming days. It's time to come out of religion, complacencies, works, luke warmness, spiritual death, and put Him as the head of your life, beyond yourself.

Imagine missing out on this great day when hordes of people come out of the great tribulation who have washed their robes. There will be a gathering in the air! We will come back on earth once He has removed the evil from the earth, and we will reign on earth for a thousand years. It's easy for me to get my head around this happening because back when Noah lived, they lived for 860 years. A thousand years is nothing with a transformed body, and this is the promise to those who have overcome.

Bless you all and I hope to see you on this great day!

The End

www.ingramcontent.com/pod-product-compliance
Lightning Source LLC
Chambersburg PA
CBHW020428010526
44118CB00010B/483